Guns, and Gunfights

Lessons and Tales from a Modern-Day Gunfighter

Guns, Bullets, and Gunfights

Lessons and Tales from a Modern-Day Gunfighter

Jim Cirillo
Paladin Press • Boulder, Colorado

Also by Jim Cirillo:

Jim Cirillo: Modern Day Gunfighter (video)
    Everything You Ever Wanted to Know About Gunfighting
    by a Guy Who Put His Life on the Line to Find Out

Secrets of a Master Gunfighter (video)
    Jim Cirillo's Advanced Guide to Combat Shooting
    and Gunfight Survival

Guns, Bullets, and Gunfights:
Lessons and Tales from a Modern-Day Gunfighter
by Jim Cirillo

Copyright © 1996 by Jim Cirillo
ISBN 0-87364-877-3
Printed in the United States of America

Published by Paladin Press, a division of
Paladin Enterprises, Inc., P.O. Box 1307,
Boulder, Colorado 80306, USA.
(303) 443-7250

Direct inquiries and/or orders to the above address.

PALADIN, PALADIN PRESS, and the "horse head" design
are trademarks belonging to Paladin Enterprises and
registered in United States Patent and Trademark Office.

All rights reserved. Except for use in a review, no
portion of this book may be reproduced in any form
without the express written permission of the publisher.

Neither the author nor the publisher assumes
any responsibility for the use or misuse of
information contained in this book.

Visit our Web site at www.paladin-press.com

Contents

PART ONE: GUNS   1

Chapter One
    AVERTING THE UNINTENTIONAL SHOT   3

Chapter Two
    HYBRID WEAPONS   9

PART TWO: BULLETS   25

Chapter Three
    THE TWO PRIMARY FUNCTIONS OF
        HANDGUN BULLETS   27

Chapter Four
    ARE HOLLOWPOINT BULLETS THE WAY
        TO GO FOR STOPPING POWER?   37

PART THREE: GUNFIGHTS   51

Chapter Five
    SELECTION OF THE GUNFIGHTER   53

Chapter Six
    SHOOTING FOR SCORE OR SURVIVAL?   61

Chapter Seven
    FIREARM TRAINING AND THE GUNFIGHT   71

Chapter Eight
    STRESS OF THE GUNFIGHT   95

Chapter Nine
    THE BIZARRE NYCPD STAKEOUT SQUAD   101
    CONCLUSION   113

WARNING

The technical data presented here, particularly on the adjustment, alteration, and use of firearms and the implementation of firearm training programs, inevitably reflect the author's beliefs and experience with specific firearms, ammunition, equipment, and techniques that the reader cannot duplicate exactly. Therefore, this information is presented for guidance only and should be approached with great caution; it is not intended to replace certified personal instruction in the handling and use of firearms and firearm ammunition. This book is offered *for academic study only*. Neither the author, publisher, or distributors of this book assumes any responsibility for the use or misuse of information contained in this book.

FOREWORD

Occasionally in one's life, events may come about that profoundly influence your future endeavors, your perspective, and your outlook on life. In early 1977, I met and became friends with Jim Cirillo. Our enduring years of friendship have taught me a lot. Jim and I have put a lot of lead downrange together, and with Jim's guidance and encouragement, I went from a tin can plinker to national champion in a few short years. Jim and I used to shoot for souvlaki sandwiches in those days, and I don't recall his ever having to buy one for me.

Jim is, in my estimation, probably the finest defensive firearms instructor that ever put a bullet in an X ring at 50 yards. He is also one of the few remaining real modern-day gunfighters. I say real because Jim is for real. His extensive record of actual gunfights while with the New York City Police Department stakeout squad is impressive, to say the least, and he has successfully blended that actual street experience with practical and competitive firearms training exercises, to the invaluable benefit of those lucky enough to have been taught by him. As a law enforcement officer with the U.S. Customs Service, when I sometimes find myself in a place where predators rule and an error in judgment or tactics could cost a life, I remember lessons learned from this firearms master and teacher of survival.

I consider myself one of the lucky ones to have been associated with Jim for so many years. Using the skills he pounded home in me, I was fortunate enough to win the 1986 National Police Revolver Championships, a milestone in my shooting career. Without Jim's inspiration and faith in me, I'd probably still be shooting tin cans today.

When remembering all the years shooting side by side with Jim—with all the disappointments, the victories, the endless experiments trying to find a better way, the questions and theories, and the endless clouds of gunsmoke in our quest for perfection—I'm always reminded of this famous quote by William Arthur Ward: "The mediocre teacher tells; the good teacher explains; the superior teacher demonstrates; the great teacher inspires." Jim inspired me, and in his book he will inspire you.

—Charles R. Grabbatin
1986 National Police Revolver Champion
U.S. Customs Service

FOREWORD

Jim Cirillo is one of the few professional firearms instructors I know who has proven himself time and time again in actual combat with some of the most dangerous criminals that ever preyed upon society—the New York City street thugs.

I first met Jim in the early 1970s at a pistol match conducted in the Hyde Park area of New York state. Jeff Cooper had arranged a combat match in conjunction with a PPC match. The combat match was broken into two stages: a night shoot and the "Mexican Defense" course.

After the smoke settled, Jim had won the PPC match and I had won the combat match. His shooting ability, along with his great sense of humor, showed me that he was my kind of guy, and I made it a point to become friends with him. During the 20 plus years that have passed since then, we have shared many great experiences and have become good friends.

Jim is a devoted husband and father, a kind and faithful friend, and an innovative designer of tactical equipment and training techniques who is dedicated to his police service background. He can be as hard as nails when it becomes necessary and has proved his mettle in many deadly situations with the worst of New York's criminal element. His ability to control himself, and the situation, during those deadly scenarios is one reason he is one of the great teachers of defensive gunfight tactics and techniques.

I will never forget my first visit with Jim in New York City. He took me on a tour through some of the most seedy sections of Manhattan. He told me with ironic humor, "If we bump into trouble, I'll toss you one of my spares." We went to Umberto's Clam House in Little Italy, and he sat me down at a special table. With a grin on his face, he told me that I was sitting in the very chair Joey Gallo was in when he was whacked by the mob.

Jim came for a visit when I first opened the Chapman Academy in Missouri, and I helped him make the transition from the revolver to the semiauto pistol. From that time on we have gained knowledge from each other that we now share with our students. There is no better way to learn practical defensive shooting tactics and techniques than from an experienced instructor who has been there. Jim Cirillo has been there.

—Ray Chapman
World Champion of Practical Shooting
Director of the Chapman Academy of Practical Shooting

PREFACE

This book is a compilation of published and unpublished articles I wrote concerning my experiences with guns, bullets, and gunfights. It is nonfiction. I only write what I feel must be said. Some of it was written in anger, some in frustration. I felt obligated to inform my readers and students that what is taught on the police academy range and in most firearms training courses is vastly different than what one will experience in actual gunfights. As you read further, it will be obvious to you how some training methods can actually contribute to the injury or death of the mistrained student.

As you read through this book, you will notice that I refer to a certain situation several times in different chapters. If you are to learn any one thing from this book, it should come from that particular situation, which I purposely speak of with redundancy. It will be the most valuable piece of information for you to absorb. There are many other useful points that you will be able to physically and mechanically apply toward the defensive use of a handgun. But it is the application of the power of the subconscious mind that I speak of throughout the book that can save your life, as it did mine. I will speak of this further in the conclusion.

—*Jim Cirillo*

Here are some of my police and shooting awards, including the DA's Award and National Championship Police Revolver Award. I ended up turning down other awards from the police department when they got chintzy and stopped offering the award and a day off as they had always done. When they began offering an award or a day off, I took the day, much to their astonishment. I would have looked like a Russian general anyway, and I had no desire to use the award points toward promotions.

The U.S. Customs Region II Pistol Team. I am at the far left. In the center is Charles Grabbatin, who became a national police revolver champion under my training.

Col. Jeff Cooper sent this novel photo to me. He called me "The Snake," and I coined the term "The Pope" for him.

I fired this "range record" target 250-18x with a Dan Wesson Model 15 with a 2 1/4-inch barrel. On my waist is the speed slide I invented, which revolutionized combat shooting. It was used by eight national police combat shooting champions.

I served as the pistol team captain for the U.S. Treasury, Federal Law Enforcement Training Center. Linda Novack (bottom row, far right) was one of my top shooters.

Acknowledgments

To two National Police Combat champions, Al Syage and Frank May of the New York City Police Department. Thank you for teaching me and encouraging me to shoot in competition. You allowed me to win my biggest prize—my life!

To my staunch stakeout parter, Bill Allard. Thank you for keeping my skin in one piece and for saving my life.

To Customs Inspector Charlie Grabbatin. Your achieving the National Police Revolver championship was the greatest compliment you gave me as your mentor.

It may seem inappropriate due to the subject matter contained in this book, but I dedicate this book to the Almighty.

It is my strong belief that it was only through divine intervention that I and my fellow police officers of the New York City Police Department Stakeout Squad miraculously escaped death so many times.

Part One

Guns

Chapter One: AVERTING THE UNINTENTIONAL SHOT

To make mistakes is only human. We have erasers on pencils and white-out for typewriters, but I have yet to see a bullet recalled after it's been fired accidentally. Of course, no one believes it can happen to them. Like herding animals, we always feel that tragedy only strikes the other animal. This thought could be the most dangerous one for the shooter to harbor, for he may very well be the "other animal."

From my own experiences and those of my peers, I have come to a very serious conclusion: the firearms fancier, collector, shooter, handler, or instructor, whether expert or not, is the most susceptible to the unintentional discharge of a firearm. Several years ago a firearms instructor and well-known pistol champion of national prominence accidentally shot and killed his wife in a tragic incident. This could very well have happened to me, as I have fired not one but three accidental shots on different occasions. I hate to admit it, but if I have to ridicule myself to get the point across, I consider myself a man for doing it. Perhaps we should form an Accidental Shooters Anonymous group so that we can meet, bare our mistakes, and compile statistics so that others may learn from us.

In my firearms safety lectures, I now include not only range safety issues but also firearms safety in the home. I describe my own mistakes to emphasize to the students that if I, a so-called "firearms expert," can make a mistake, then so can they. I do not leave them with the impression that there is no hope, but I do put the fear in them so that whenever they touch a weapon, they know that there is potential for an accidental discharge. Then I suggest how we can put erasers on the end of gun muzzles.

I start by telling them that in every accidental shot (I mean every *truly* accidental shot), the shooter swore the weapon was empty. So we now can conclude that the most dangerous weapon is the "empty" one, and this is the weapon we should fear the most. If I can instill absolute fear in the student of an empty weapon or an assumed empty weapon, the "empty weapon" shooting phenomenon should decrease.

If my students by now have it ingrained in them that there is always the potential that any firearm can discharge during handling, how can they minimize this danger? Here I tell them to pick a safe spot in their homes for weapons handling.

This area must have some prerequisite features. It should have a solid bullet-stopping construction, such as an outer brick or masonry wall. If the student lives in a wood frame house, a chimney or a fireplace is suitable. If this is not available, a stove, refrigerator, sink, or tub could act as an emergency stop for handgun bullets. An accidental shot here can be repaired with spackle, putty, auto body fiberglass, or epoxy and paint. There also should be no thoroughfare between the solid bullet stop and the place where the weapon will be handled. A controlled entrance into the weapons-handling area is desirable as well.

Another important aspect of safety concerns the student's

I believe in familiarizing family members with all aspects of a weapon and allowing children of a reasonable age to handle a weapon under supervision to remove the curiosity all children have about handguns. Once the curiosity is satisfied, most children will not seek out the firearm, but you must still secure the weapon as an additional hedge against the unintended shot.

weapon and the immediate family. This is a facet of weapons safety that is rarely mentioned or only touched upon. There are many serious implications if the wrong information is given, so many firearms instructors cop out and simply tell students that they must safeguard their weapons from family members and leave it at that. This minimal advice could lead to a tragedy.

My personal method, and one I pass on to my trainees, is to totally familiarize the whole family with the weapon, especially children who are old enough to comprehend. Any child who can fire a weapon should be familiarized with it. I feel that if you satisfy the curiosity of the child and then go a step further and instruct that child in safe weapon handling, then he or she should be allowed to see and handle the firearm under supervision whenever he or she wishes. This can be a bother in the beginning, but the novelty will soon wear off as the curiosity is alleviated. The child will probably break your horns for about a week asking to see the weapon, but after that the gun, which is available to handle and see, is no longer a mysterious thrill. It now becomes more like a piece of furniture, about as interesting as a table lamp.

I know of two cases, one tragic and one amusing but almost tragic, where family members handling a law enforcement officer's weapon caused problems. The amusing story was told to me by one of my firearms instructors who felt the same as I did about familiarizing family members with his weapons. He was amazed when he first heard my firearms safety lecture since he had never heard the theory of familiarization in the home at any other such lecture.

In this case he had shown his 4-year-old son all aspects of handling his S&W Model 60. One night while he was watching television on his brand-new 21-inch color set, into the living room walks his proud little son with his father's cocked revolver. Before Ray realized what his son held in his hand, junior stated, "Daddy, I am going to shoot the bad guys on television." At this point, he didn't know whether to hit the deck, try to grab the revolver, or just let it happen while safely out of the way. Just as Ray shouted, "No, don't shoot the gun," his son, holding the gun in an almost perfect Weaver stance just like daddy showed him, squeezed the trigger. As Ray cringed, waiting for the blast and wondering if his insurance would cover a bullet hole in his color picture tube, he heard a dull metallic click. Little Ray's voice then spoke, "It's alright, daddy. I took the bullets out like you showed me!"

Here was one potential tragedy averted due to the familiarization of a family member. Needless to say, little Ray did not sit too comfortably for several days, but now he will ask before he touches daddy's gun.

The second incident was a terrible tragedy. In this case the law enforcement officer was taught the standard "hide your weapon and never show it to anyone," including family members. But the officer's wife found his revolver in her 7-year-old son's drawer, and it was cocked! Not wanting her son to touch it, she picked it up immediately and went to find her husband so he could disarm it. He was napping on the couch in the living room as she approached him, cocked gun and fresh linen in her hands. Struck with the clumsiness that overtakes some people in fear, she dropped a pillowcase, reached for it, and at that instant the weapon discharged. The police officer never awoke from his nap.

Looking at this incident, it's easy to see how all the pieces came together. The officer's curious 7-year-old sees daddy sleeping, finds the mysterious revolver, takes it to his room to examine it, cocks it, hears his mother coming into the room to replenish his linen, opens his dresser draw, and hides it among his linen, where his mother finds it. Result: the end of a happy family. Family familiarization with the gun would have prevented this tragedy.

Once the family is totally familiarized with any weapon in the house and is given the same safety lecture that the law enforcement officer received, and once each member can handle the weapon with utmost safety, it does not mean that the officer can now leave his weapon accessible and lying about. He must still take steps to safeguard it. Familiarization is only a safeguard in the event that the weapon, perhaps out of haste or forgetfulness, is left in plain sight of family members. Now they will carefully—not carelessly or curiously—handle it.

If someone in your family is under medical care, is taking medication or drugs, or has some psychological problem, the weapon must be safeguarded. There is no way to predict how someone's mind is working when, for example, they know they have a dreaded terminal disease. I had one of my trainee's fathers, who was a retired law enforcement officer, kill himself with his son's service gun, knowing full well the predicament he would place his son in. In another case, a female law enforcement officer had just returned from her honeymoon. She was in the kitchen cooking and her husband was in the living room signing thank-you cards for the wedding gifts. His pen ran dry, so he called to his wife for another. She replied that there was one in her handbag. A few moments later she heard a muffled shot. She ran into the living room and found her husband with the top of his head blown off. Her off-duty weapon was also in the handbag.

Was it suicide? A foolish act? Did he toy with the gun and

get caught with an unintended shot, or did his mind snap for just a moment? No one knows. This case, I am sure, was one of those rare weird occurrences.

I know most safety lectures are boring, and most people feel they do not need them. It would have been much easier for me to write about some of my gunfights or adventures in the New York City Police Department, but that will come later in the book. My conscience dictates that I first must try to increase your safety awareness. After all, I want to keep you around long enough to read my future articles and books! So remember, *never* consider a weapon empty, *only* point it where you wish to fire, and safeguard it *after* you have familiarized your people with it.

Chapter Two: HYBRID WEAPONS

In the past, almost all shooters accepted a handgun as it came out of the factory, except for a few pros who insisted on special sights and grips and perhaps a trigger and action job. About 25 years ago, in the interest of obtaining a higher score on the then so-called Practical Police Course (PPC), I came up with a hybrid modification on a pistol that I am not proud of. I took my idea to pistolsmith Austin Behlert and asked him if he could take a .358 rifle barrel and make a bull barrel to fit my K38 Smith & Wesson. He said he could and also suggested he could fit a Bo-Mar rib, then made for 1911 .45 slides, to fit the top of the pistol barrel. This modification, due to the extra weight, allowed me a head-hold aiming point on the B27 silhouette target.

Wow, did my scores climb! I was one of the first police shooters in the northeast to shoot a 599 out of a possible 600 on the National Rifle Association PPC course. The very next day after I shot that score, there was a mad rush to the gunsmiths. I never dreamed that my hybrid revolver would start the customized police revolver industry and, at the same time, degenerate the Practical Police Course. If a police officer carried this modification as fired in the now-named NRA Police Revolver Course, his pants would fall down after about one hour on duty. (I am glad they got honest and changed the name to the Police Revolver Course, as there is no way that the course is practical.)

Now don't get me wrong! I don't mean to imply that all customizations or modifications on pistols are wrong. But as with the Police Revolver Course, practical shooting in the interest of higher competition scores is getting warped and degenerating away from true practical applications of gunfight principles.

On the left are a factory .41 Magnum Dan Wesson (top) and Smith & Wesson Model 57 .41 Magnum (bottom). On the right are my hybrid Smith & Dans: a .41 Magnum Dan Wesson barrel and shroud fitted to a Smith & Wesson Model 57 frame (top) and a Dan Wesson .44 Magnum barrel and shroud fitted with a Bo-Mar rib on a S&W Model 29.

Competitors, or should I say gamesmen, are always looking for gimmicks like pin guns and trick holsters to improve their scores.

This, however, could be an asset as well. If one develops a modification that increases performance while maintaining practical application, he is cooking with gas. This type of improvement should always be encouraged. A good example is what Charles Kelsey did with the Devel version of the S&W Models 39 and 59. He reduced their overall size, aiding their concealability, and increased their reliability and accuracy. Another plus was Larry Kelley's Magna-Port on .357 and .44 Magnums, which helped cut down muzzle flip and allowed for faster follow-up shots.

After engaging in several firefights as a member of the NYCPD Stakeout Squad, I opted to use a weapon that allowed a greater application of power than the standard police .38 Special. At that time, a 158-grain round-nose lead police load only achieved 747 feet per second (fps) out of a 4-inch barrel. Even accurate heart shots were not instant stoppers. These poor results gave birth to two of my hybrids. I refitted a Model 10 .38 frame with a Model 19 .357 cylinder and a 4-inch Douglas barrel. I then fitted a Bo-Mar rib over the barrel. This hybrid allowed me to shoot accurately and fast with close to .357 power. I used a home-brewed special load—a 125-grain cup-point half-jacketed wadcutter traveling between 1,250 and

I do not want readers to get the impression that I only support the use of stock weapons. I support any modification that improves performance and can still be used in a practical manner. Here is a 1911A1 .45 modified by Crawford Guns of Altha, Florida. Its compensated barrel allows for great control of rapid repeat shots, making this weapon desirable for gunfighting.

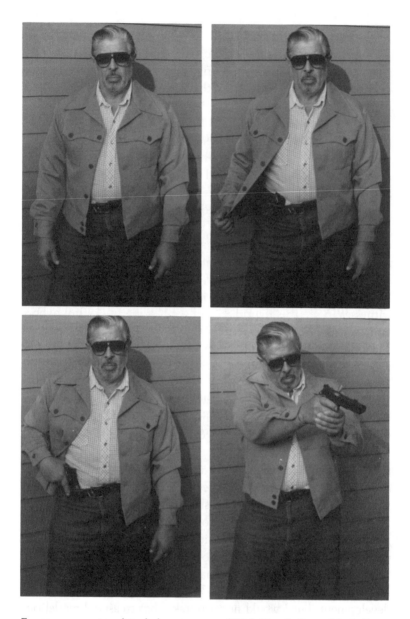

Even a cop wearing plainclothes can conceal Dick Crawford's modified .45 and deploy it readily.

1,300 fps. I went to a flat-edge cup point due to the fact that in many confrontations, I was only offered head shots—the gunmen who did not give up when challenged generally ducked for cover, leaving only their heads or a portion of their heads for a target.

I had first used Super Vel 110-grain semiwadcutter hollowpoints, but in some cases the semiwadcutter's ogive shape only allowed the bullet to penetrate the scalp and skid off the skull. My sharp-edge cup points would dig in. When I tested them on auto body metal, the cup points would pierce with a considerably sharp angle of entry. The one big advantage the revolver has over the auto pistol is that one can use this type of bullet configuration reliably without malfunction.

I am working on a special auto cartridge that will allow the same advantage, especially with the 10mm, .45 ACP, and .38 Super. Mas Ayoob was one of the first patent-disclosure witnesses to see this hybrid. I fired a magazine full of my hybrid bullets through a standard 1911 .45 with an unaltered magazine. They flowed through the action better than GI ball and made eight full .45-caliber wadcutter holes on the target. I never saw Massad's eyes open so wide.

My other hybrid weapons were developed as a result of my hunting. I love to hunt big game with a pistol, but I hate to sight in with a standard Smith & Wesson Model 29 using full .44 Magnum power. The hand sting and recoil always bothered me. My wife also hunts with me. She uses one of my long-distance stakeout weapons, a scoped Model 27 .357 Magnum with an 8 3/8-inch barrel, and she has popped seven deer with it. I had used that gun prior to obtaining my Model 29 for deer hunting, but I put the 29 aside when I received the first production Model 44 Dan Wesson.

The Dan Wesson people had given me one of the original handmade 44s, serial number X43, for the help I gave them in its development, but I would not dare take that treasured model out in the field. I ended up giving the production model to my wife, as you can shoot it all day long without discomfort. She had wanted a more powerful weapon ever since a big buck made it seven miles after she hit it with the .357 Smith & Wesson Model 27.

I got some nice young spike camp meat with my hybrid Smith & Dan .44 Magnum. I always hunt big game with a handgun.

My wife, Mildred, took this huge doe with a .44 Magnum Dan Wesson. The doe is standing on the ground and is 2 feet higher than my 5' 9 1/2". I am glad I taught Mildred to shoot, as she has brought home the bacon many times. She shot this deer in the neck from a 15-foot tree stand at 70 paces.

I reluctantly went back to the Smith & Wesson Model 29, and I hated every shot I made with it. Then my wife complained that the Dan Wesson was too heavy for quick shots. She liked it to shoot while on a supported stand but missed jump shots with it.

I pondered the two problems, and this gave life to a new hybrid. I called the Dan Wesson people and told them of my plan for the gun. Since they are a progressive bunch, they sent me a 6-inch ported .44 Mag barrel and a 4-inch shroud. I had the receiver threads cut off the barrel, then had my gunsmith rethread it for my S&W Model 29 frame. I installed the Dan Wesson barrel and shroud onto the 29 and machine grooved a Bo-Mar rib and fitted that to the Dan Wesson shroud rib.

What a honey of a hybrid! It's light enough for my wife to handle and carry yet heavy enough in combination with the ported barrel to tame recoil, and it's more accurate than the original 29 barrel. If I'd only had this weapon during my stakeout days, I could have chipped down the odds even more than I did.

If I were back doing stakeouts, my hybrid Smith & Dan (the Model 29 Smith & Wesson with the Dan Wesson shroud and barrel) would be my choice for a carry weapon. Of course, I would load it with a 185-grain Cirillo cup-point wadcutter and send it out at around 1,500 fps.

Some may say that a Model 29 with a 4-inch barrel is too much gun to carry. To them I say, you will quickly change your mind when you get into a gunfight and see your opponent staring at you intently and raising his weapon toward you. As you fire, you can see the flash of your gunfire in the reflection of his eyes, and in those fractions of a second, which seem like an eternity, you will hear your own voice asking yourself, "Why don't those eyes flutter and close? Why doesn't he fall? Will he fire and hit me? Will I die?" It's then you will wish you had a hand cannon that will part your opponent in quarters with one shot. If you do get into that kind of situation, I am sure you will join me and say, "Yeah, that Model 29 is just fine to carry!"

I planned another hybrid when my son joined the police department. He followed in my footsteps and carried the very same badge with all the nicks and scars and dents I obtained from my 23 years of New York City police duty. He has since

My hybrid .44 Magnum Smith & Wesson Model 29 with a Dan Wesson ported barrel and shroud and Bo-Mar rib and sight installed. If I knew I was going to be in a gunfight, this is the weapon I would choose. I was developing it for stakeouts, but the unit was disbanded before I was able to use it. My special .44 Magnum wadcutters are alongside the weapon.

added a few of his own. I figured if he were to be thrust into a high-firefight squad such as the one I was in, I would want him to have the most useful weapon possible.

I made a hybrid out of a Smith & Wesson Model 57 .41 Magnum using the same technique of putting a Dan Wesson barrel and shroud onto the S&W frame. In the interest of experimentation, I did not add a Bo-Mar rib but tried a 6-inch barrel instead. This weapon showed great promise. I was shocked during my first test using W/W Silvertips in .41 Magnum. I thought Winchester Western had given me bum ammo. It shot with excellent accuracy, but I doubted its power. The next day, I took out the chronograph. Again, I was shocked. The graph read 1,275 fps with the W/W 175 Silvertip. I could have sworn it would read 820 or 850 fps, as its felt recoil was exactly like .38 Special +P out of a 4-inch Model 10.

I then fired the Silvertip out of a standard Smith &

This conversion on a Model 57 with a Dan Wesson barrel and shroud makes shooting 175-grain Silvertips in .41 Magnum feel like .38 Special 158-grain ball service loads. I thought I had weak ammo until I ran it on a chronograph and was surprised to see that the Silvertip had given out 1,250 fps. I feel the .41 Magnum is a highly underrated police round.

Wesson Model 57 .41 Magnum to see if the mild recoil was mostly due to the W/W Silvertips. Again, I was totally surprised. The recoil was comparable to just under standard .357 power. While this was respectable, it was still a far cry from the Smith & Dan hybrid that gave only .38 Special +P felt recoil.

The .41 hybrid's accuracy was a repeat of the .44 Smith & Dan—the Dan Wesson barrel outshot the original Smith & Wesson barrel. The Dan Wesson .41 barrels are not ported like the .44 Mag barrels. The weight of the hybrid Dan Wesson .41 Magnum barrel and Model 57 frame firing the .41 Magnum ammo balances out for very comfortable handling. Shooting a Dan Wesson Model 57 with W/W .41 Magnum Silvertips felt almost like shooting .38 Special mid-range loads out of a K38.

The straight Dan Wesson models are perfectly designed for shooting the powerful .44 and .41 Magnum loads. They are great for hunting, silhouette, and sport shooting but are too heavy for fast-handling police use unless you are about 6'4" and weigh over 300 pounds! The Smith & Wesson N frames are just too light for .41 and .44 Mag police use.

If someone were smart, he would buy up or produce Dan Wesson barrels and shrouds just for conversions of standard revolvers, especially now that Dan Wesson is out of business. Note the smooth match of the S&W frame and Dan Wesson shroud.

On the other hand, the Cirillo hybrid of the S&W N frame and the Dan Wesson shroud and barrel shooting either the .41 and .44 Magnum is a plausible police weapon. Now we have a weapon that is heavy enough to tame a powerful cartridge and yet not too heavy to carry into a firefight.

Now, how many of you handgun hunters reading this still have your Model 29 accumulating dust? You have two choices: 1) sell it and buy a Dan Wesson, or 2) buy a Dan Wesson barrel and shroud and convert it into a shooting weapon you can handle. Both choices should be of comparable cost. If you elect to convert, remember you can change barrels or barrel length at will. Any machinist or gunsmith can do it. First, cut and rethread the Dan Wesson barrel, then index the shroud to the frame. Purchase a barrel 2 inches longer than the shroud or a shroud 2 inches shorter than the barrel, a barrel nut, and a Dan Wesson installation tool from the Dan Wesson Company. Retail cost at the time of this writing is about $160.

I would like to see Dan Wesson conversion kits for .41 and

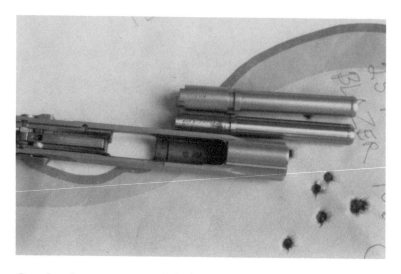

One of my favorite conversion hybrids: a Model 1066 10mm slide and barrel alongside Irv Stone's Bar-Sto barrel made in .40 S&W to fit the 1066. I feel the .40 S&W cartridge should not be made to shoot in 9mm frames. I prefer the larger 1066 or 1046 frame. I did the same by putting a .40 S&W barrel by Jarvis on a Model 20 Glock.

.44 Magnum already threaded so it would be a simple task for a gunsmith to remove your Smith or Ruger barrel and install a superaccurate Dan Wesson barrel. This would cut your costs down, but believe me, whatever the cost it is worth it. You would be achieving several improvements, including greater accuracy (the Wesson barrel is supported on both ends and under tension, which stops barrel whip and is probably one of the reasons Wesson barrels and pistols are noted for excellent accuracy) and reduced recoil due to a heavy shroud as well as the gas porting on the .44 Mag. You can also easily change barrel lengths to suit your purpose. (As this book went to press, I sadly learned that the Dan Wesson Company had gone into bankruptcy. I hope someone will start it up again or at least produce the barrels and shrouds to adopt to other firearms as conversion kits.)

Many of my co-workers at the Federal Law Enforcement Training Center fell in love with my hybrid Smith & Dan Wesson handgun and are anxiously awaiting

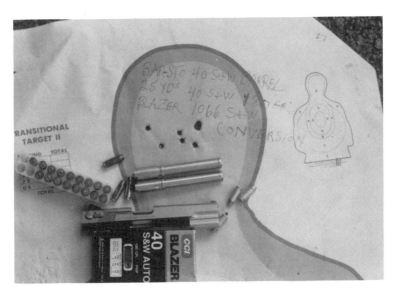

A group shot with the Bar-Sto .40 S&W barrel made by Irv Stone for my Model 1066. The group would have been much tighter, but I was anxious to shoot this new conversion while still recovering from Lyme disease contracted from a tick bite while on a hunting trip.

A student shooting my Glock Model 21 with an Alchemy drop-in barrel and compensator. Note the 10mm brass suspended just above the ejection port and the absence of recoil.

HYBRID WEAPONS

Dick Crawford of Crawford Guns putting a sight cut on one of my slides. I prefer using a gunsmith who's a shooter, as he knows what a shooter wants. Dick holds many shooting records and was on the All-Guard Team, breaking the high 2,600 score many times. He has broken international records as well and recently won the High Senior Award at the 1995 Bianchi Shoot.

Wesson barrel conversion kits. I guarantee that if any of you try a Wesson barrel conversion on your weapon, you will thank me for suggesting it.

Part Two
Bullets

Chapter Three
THE TWO PRIMARY FUNCTIONS OF HANDGUN BULLETS

It should be a simple matter of deduction to list the primary functions of handgun bullets. Of course there are always people, some of them in high places, who can totally confuse the issue. Take, for instance, a former surgeon general, who made the profound statement, "We should be thinking about making safer guns and safer ammunition." Whatever that means is beyond my comprehension. The Geneva Conventions declared that only full-metal-jacket ammo could be used in warfare between nations. What does this actually mean when land mines, hand grenades, artillery fragmentation shells, and flamethrowers are okay?

When I was a firearms instructor with the New York City Police Department (NYCPD), I suggested that the 158-grain round-nose lead bullet was totally ineffective for stopping dangerous criminals. In many cases it caused injury or death to bystanders due to its ricochet potential and penetrating ability. I stated that we should consider using expanding hollowpoint bullets. My superior in charge of the firearms unit replied, "Oh, we can't do that. That's cruel and inhumane."

My God, we could only use a firearm when our lives or limbs were in imminent danger, and he was telling me that I must shoot the criminal nicely, without too much gore and blood! No wonder so many New York cops get killed even after they shoot first. Believe it or not, unless they've changed recently, New York City police officers are now carrying full-metal jacket 9mm loads in their sidearms. It's a good thing they reversed the 10-shot limit in their magazines, because the cops are going to need plenty of ammo to put their man down before all those tiny perforations take effect. If they don't wise up and change, watch the civilian casualties build up—and the lawsuits.

It's obvious that the reason we have such ludicrous rules is because those who make those rules have never been in a gunfight. I'm sure if they had been in some of the gunfights that I was in, they would be screaming for exploding bullets! I have seen felons get shot with 158-grain .38 Special, 200- and 230-grain .45 ACP, 115-grain 9mm hollowpoints, 110-grain .30 Carbine softpoint, 55-grain .223 Remington, 12-gauge 00 buck magnum, and 12-gauge 1-ounce slugs, and only two of those incidents were one-shot stops. And all of the above bullets had at least one or two of the primary functions needed for stopping power.

By now you must be asking, "Hey, Cirillo, what the heck are the functions you're talking about?" It's very simple. It all relates to your intended target.

The first function is accuracy. How much accuracy, you ask? I would accept hand-held 4- to 5-inch groups at 25 yards. I say this because in some of my gunfights, all that was afforded as a target was the head or part of the head as the gunmen ducked behind the victims and used them as shields. So if I can hit a portion of a head out to 25 yards, I know I can easily hit a head well within 25 yards.

The rationale about head shots at 25 yards pertains mainly

to law enforcement. A civilian can accept a larger group, I would say 8 to 10 inches or perhaps a bit more, out to 25 yards. In most cases a civilian should not shoot at 25 yards or more. At that distance, legally he should be seeking cover or running. Statistics show that if you are confronted by an armed adversary at 25 yards, the chances of your getting hit are less than 3 to 5 percent.

I know that statement gets your dander and macho up. I know you feel you don't want the SOB to get away with the crap he's pulling. But my reason for making that statement is twofold. Number one, you are not sworn to endanger your life to apprehend a dangerous criminal, nor are you paid to do it. And number two, I feel you should use exotic ammo with lots of stopping power in defense of your life, and I have found that this type of ammo only has acceptable accuracy at close distances. And close distances are all you should be concerned with, since the closer you are to your adversary the more danger you are in.

So the first function of a handgun bullet is that it has the necessary inherent accuracy for the distances required. We establish the requirements for handgun ammo accuracy based on geographical considerations. For police it's 25+ yards. For civilians in an urban setting, within 10 yards is acceptable accuracy. Civilians in rural areas probably should have at least 50-yard accuracy ability.

Have you figured out the second primary function of handgun bullets? This one should be obvious. If you said it should stop or destroy the intended target, you're right. Of course, law enforcement, the National Rifle Association, and liberals shy away from the term "destroy." They prefer "hit the target." I disagree with this soft pedal, as more U.S. citizens possess handguns for protection than they do for target practice, and I am not even including handgun hunters who need the same amount of stopping power as those who use handguns for personal protection. I am sorry if I offend or disgust those who oppose my terminology and approach, but the fact is there is no way to shoot someone nicely.

This second primary function of a handgun bullet is controversial. What translates into stopping power or, more realistically, what will destroy the target best? Stopping power comes from the handgun bullet's ability to destroy as much of the portion of the target it strikes. This destruction should occur as deep into the target as possible, and it should be in as wide an area around the bullet path as possible.

The problem is how to achieve the most destructive bullet path. As I stated previously, this is highly controversial. Some theories state that light, high-velocity, expanding bullets will achieve this, while others state that large-diameter heavy bullets will. My contention is that both may be right, while in some cases both may be wrong.

I know this sounds like a riddle, but the statement is true. Let's start with high-speed, lightweight bullets. I know of a test done on live pigs. The military, using the Glaser Safety Slug in .357 and 9mm, recorded dramatic instant kills on the pigs. But there was only one problem. Were the pigs dressed like someone living in St. Paul, Minnesota, in the dead of winter with a wallet full of credit cards in his Mackinaw pocket? Yes, I can understand an instant kill on a bare pig or possibly one with a thin summer shirt on, but other real-world issues such as how a criminal might be dressed must be considered. There is no panacea bullet that can handle all conditions.

Some of you may feel that the Glaser Safety Slug or similarly constructed bullets expand too readily when used against heavy clothing or leather, defeating their desired effect. You may think a controlled-expansion bullet such as a Black Talon hollowpoint would be better in winter conditions. My findings are that the controlled-expansion hollowpoints are defeated sometimes if the hollowpoint cavity plugs up with clothing and debris. These rounds need a noncompressible liquid like blood or body fluids in order to expand reliably. A plugged-up hollowpoint acts like a standard pointy bullet and just pierces with a small wound.

Controlled-expansion hollowpoints may expand more readily after passing through light clothing. I've found that this expansion occurs within only the first 2 inches of entry in body tissue. After that, expanding hollowpoint bullets fold back into a round mushroom shape and act like slightly larger round-nose bullets.

Any bullet with a round nose or ogive will only part tissue, causing a wound channel smaller then the bullet's diameter, because as the bullet passes, the parted tissue closes. This prevents rapid blood loss while slowing neurological shock. The forensic experts I have questioned while attending many postmortem examinations stated that they couldn't tell the difference between a .32 caliber round-nose bullet and a .45 round-nose if both had passed through the body, since both only make small wound channels as they pass through tissue.

The only way that a light high-velocity bullet will cause enough destruction is if its configuration and construction are combined with high enough velocity. By this I mean that the Glaser, with its prefragmented bullet, will do its job against light clothing if it's fired out of a handgun that gives it high velocity. If we can get the velocity high enough, a jacketed soft-nose will also cause sufficient wound destruction. We had a good number of one-shot stops with a specialized .30 carbine firing a 110-grain softpoint bullet traveling close to 1,900 fps. If we tried to get this velocity with a 110-grain bullet out of a handgun, the recoil would have been too excessive. A heavy .357 pistol shooting 125-grain hollowpoints at more than 1,500 fps should give fair results in moderate weather.

Again, in St. Paul in the winter, I would go to a heavier caliber. Now this heavier caliber and bullet will not do the job in St. Paul in the winter, or in Florida in the summer for that matter, if its construction or configuration is not right. The 230-grain round-nose .45 ACP has been touted by many as the ultimate load, but I know of several cases where gunmen ran away after being hit square with this round.

I know of an amusing occurrence told to me by my buddy Tom Campbell of IPSC fame. While he was with the U.S. shooting team in Africa, he was hunting as a guest with the late Kirk Kirkham, who was also on the U.S. team. Kirk spotted a dik dik, a small antelope about the size of a medium-sized dog. Kirk whispered, "Camp meat, Tom," lined up his sights on his 1911A1, and squeezed off a .45 ACP hardball round. While continuing to chew grass, the dik dik raised his head, looked both ways, and preceded to lower his head and resume feeding.

Kirk, embarrassed, took more careful aim and fired a second shot. At this, the dik dik jumped up and started to run off wobbly. The host escort quickly raised his rifle and finished the animal off with a massive rear end shot. Amazed, Kirk ran up and turned the little antelope over. Sure enough, there were two holes, side by side, in the dik dik's rib cage. He looked up at Tom and asked, "How could this be?" Tom replied, "Oh, I guess he never read Jeff Cooper's red book."

Believe it or not, I have also seen this phenomenon both on deer I have hunted and on men shot through the rib cage with 12-gauge slugs. I know it's hard to believe, but think about what I said before. A 1-ounce 12-gauge slug, even though it is close to 60 caliber, still has an ogive (a round nose). As I said before, even a large, heavy bullet is not always effective if its construction or configuration does not impart destruction.

In the dik dik's case, a 9mm Glaser would have done the job if Kirk had been close enough to take advantage of the round's velocity and accuracy. A large, heavy caliber also would have dispatched the animal if the bullet had a full-diameter .45-caliber sharp wadcutter profile. This would have created a .45-caliber entrance hole, allowing air into the chest cavity, and a full .45-caliber cut through the lung tissue. This combination of heavy internal bleeding and the vacuum loss in the rib cage due to the open .45-caliber wound would have caused a pneumothorax, suffocating the dik dik quickly—that is if neuro shock didn't drop him first.

Dr. Martin Fackler, the noted wound ballistic expert, is also of the opinion that a full bullet diameter with a hard outer edge nose in full wadcutter is the best configuration for an efficient destructive wound channel. The only problem with this configuration is that presently only a revolver can successfully shoot this type of bullet repeatedly. In a semiautomatic pistol, only the first bullet placed into the chamber by hand will work; then only standard semiauto rounds can be used to feed behind it.

During one of my stakeout confrontations, my partner, Bill Allard, saved my butt using this very combination. When I came out of our position to confront the robbers, a group of

Ed Sanow tested and wrote about my patented bullets for *Handguns* magazine. Ed told me that my bullet created the largest permanent wound channel of any bullet he ever tested.

hotel guests appeared directly behind the gunmen. I did not dare fire with innocents in the background. The first gunman raised his pistol toward my face. Then from the side of my vision I saw a cloud of dust, smoke, and particles and then heard the wonderful sound of Bill's 1911A1 .45 Colt. Earlier that day I had hand-swaged a 200-grain .45 ACP full wadcutter in my basement workshop at home and loaded it with 7.7 grains of Unique powder. I had hand-placed this round in the chamber of Bill's Colt, then backed it with a magazine of seven semi-wadcutter hollowpoints. The .45 ACP wadcutter stopped the robber in his tracks, and he was dead before he hit the hotel lobby floor.

The next day, Bill and I were happy to rush over to the

Bellevue Morgue. (This was required after every shooting to help the forensic people recreate the sequence of events during the autopsy.) The pathologists looked at us with cocked eyes. They had never seen cops who were so anxious to witness the gory autopsy. Little did they know we were experimenting with bullets and were anxious to see how effective my home-swaged .45 wadcutters were. (I later found out they nicknamed us "the Ghouls.")

After I saw how well they worked, I tried to figure out a way to get them to feed in semiauto pistols, as I wanted Bill to be able to shoot full wadcutters reliably. (I used revolvers, so I had no problem.) After much experimenting I solved the problem. In fact, they worked so well I decided to take out a patent. Since then I have successfully shot full wadcutters with the most obtrusive nose I could find in .38 Super, 10mm, 40 S&W, and most successfully in .45 ACP. When Ed Sanow was contracted by a publishing firm to test and write about my

Bill Kaswer was extremely helpful in testing my bullet concept. My bullet testing during federal service showed me that Felon Grabber bullets were the best commercial bullets available for wounding ability. That is why I asked Bill to make Pin Grabbers in full diameter. Bill asked, "How the hell are you going to get them to work through an auto action?" I replied, "That's my problem."

patented bullets, he told me that my .45 ACP made the largest wound channel of any bullet he had ever tested. I only hope I can get a company to pick up my patent so we can get them made commercially. Until then, I like Cor-Bon's .40 and .45 +P, Federal's 9mm +P+, Bill Kaswer's various Pin or Felon Grabbers, and Triton's +P loads.

I do not want readers to get the impression that the right bullet design or caliber is all that is needed to achieve stopping power. Do not fool yourself into thinking you can handle anything that comes your way just because you have the most potent, exotic bullets made. Never forget one of the most important factors of all: *proper bullet placement* with a standard bullet can stop a gunfight quicker then the most powerful exotic bullet that is not properly placed. So please, practice excellent bullet placement before buying that exotic load. I hope to get to greet each one of you from time to time at various shooting ranges—right after you've finished your bullet placement practice.

Chapter Four

ARE HOLLOWPOINT BULLETS THE WAY TO GO FOR STOPPING POWER?

This subject of handgun bullet stopping power will probably be controversial long after Jim Cirillo goes to the big shoot-out in the sky. I have been involved with this subject since my early days with the New York City Police Department. In the late 1950s, as a rookie police officer, I hated the pointy-nose lead 158-grain .38 Special we were required to carry. It was obvious to me even without much firearms knowledge that a pointy, solid bullet would fully penetrate a target, making only a small self-sealing hole and perhaps hitting some innocent victim in the background. Sure enough, this happened time and time again.

A secondary problem was that even when police officers fired with good accuracy and penetrated a felon's heart, the

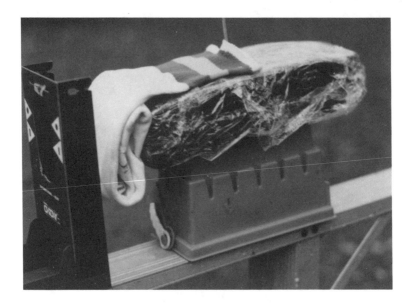

I test all bullets by shooting through folded heavy hunting socks to simulate clothing on tissue. Note the chronograph just before the collagen block.

Right: Preparing test medium of animal collagen for a bullet test.

felon was sometimes still able to get off several shots, killing the police officer prior to his own slow death from the officer's bullet. It was not until the 1970s that the poor performance of the .38 Special police load was realized. It was brought to light that a solid-point projectile traveling at the slow velocity of 750 fps did not disrupt tissue and penetrated deeply as a result. The configuration of a point only parted tissue and allowed the wound to close and seal quickly, preventing full blood loss.

When I was assigned to the stakeout squad, I disobeyed department orders and purposely used .38 Special 110-grain Super-Vel JHP bullets that Lee Jurras had made for me. I had chronographed these special bullets at Al Dinan's shop, and his chronograph read 1,125 fps out of my 4-inch Model 10 Smith & Wesson. I knew I would be involved in gun battles in crowded supermarkets or banks, and I wanted my bullets to stay within my intended targets. The Super-Vel round had a decent

ARE HOLLOWPOINTS THE WAY TO GO?

My patented bullet with guide nose attached. Bill Kaswer made .45 ACP wadcutters in Pin Grabber configuration for my bullets. I then applied the guide nose and loaded the round.

Using Bill Kaswer's sample Pin Grabbers in a full wadcutter, I could show that the most obstrusive configuration would work through autos with my concept. Note how the slot allows the bullet to divide into a flat, wide expansion.

My patented bullet with guide nose disassembled. During firing, as the bullet nose projects past the muzzle, the centrifugal force pulls apart the guide nose while the back half of the bullet is still on the rifling, allowing it to maintain accuracy unimpeded by the guide nose.

My bullets in 10mm. Note the unfinished rounds showing the expansion slots and the partially disassembled guide nose (right) to show how the patent works.

hollowpoint with a light copper jacket that allowed for sufficient velocity and good tissue disruption. This combination almost always resulted in an expanded bullet that stayed within body tissue.

After my first gun battle using Super-Vels, I became aware of another important factor in the selection of a bullet: configuration. The Super-Vel bullet had a semiwadcutter shape with a rather tapered ogive nose configuration. On body hits, its construction usually caused a fair amount of tissue destruction. In this particular firefight, however, one of the felons ducked down as he ran toward the cashier. He probably wanted to use her as a hostage shield. Only the top of his head was exposed above the display shelves of the store. I fired three shots at his exposed head before he dropped from sight.

At the postmortem the next day, it was evident how he was able to get off one shot during our gunfire exchange—my first two bullets only pierced the scalp, skidded around the skull, and emerged. Only one bullet had penetrated the skull and entered the brain. (Luckily, his bullet struck the shelves laden with canned goods in front of me. He could have just as easily hit me if he had shot 4 inches higher.)

The other two felons were able to run out of the store and escape in a waiting vehicle. They were picked up by the local precinct officers when a doctor's office called the police about two men with severe bullet wounds. Later, when the officers met us, one asked, "What the hell did you shoot those guys with? Every bullet hole in them was the size of a quarter." So I was satisfied with the results of the body hits with the Super-Vel but somewhat disappointed with the hits on the felon that I head shot.

Over the next few weeks, you couldn't get Jim Cirillo out of his basement. I was shooting every bullet round conceivable in all kinds of tests with all kinds of reloads I could think of. I liked the ballistics of the Lee Jurras rounds; they provided good recoil control with a fair amount of stopping power, except for the unpredictable results when head shots were called for. This worried me, as in that gunfight the holdup man was partially covered by store shelves, exposing only his head and shoulders. I knew I needed a round I could rely on that would not skid off a skull.

Using auto body metal as a test medium, I experimented with various bullets, including full jacketed, flat nose, and hollowpoints. They all penetrated well when shot close to right angles, but I noticed that the more ogive a bullet had, the more it skidded off the metal when fired from an oblique angle. This was true even with some Super-Vels. All of a sudden I got the bright idea of pulling a Super-Vel bullet, inverting it, and reseating it. I now had a full diameter, full-jacketed, sharp-corner wadcutter.

Wow! What a fantastic penetrater this configuration became. I could hardly get it to skid off the auto body metal no matter how much I angled the shot. This modification worked

My testing showed that a sharp-perimeter nose on a full wadcutter bullet with a center slot instead of a hollowpoint created the most damage in simulated tissue made of collagen. I believe that the limited velocity of handgun bullets does not create enough tissue damage by hydrostatic shock. Handgun bullets can only create damage (related to stopping power) by mechanical means with the proper configuration and construction.

In every test I made shooting into simulated tissue, my patented bullet expanded to 1 inch and always created a massive wound channel.

I believe that, with the proper configuration and construction, the bigger bullet can outperform the smaller bullet even if its configuration and construction are thought to be proper as well. Comparing this with the previous two photos, it is quite evident which bullet will be more effective.

well within 10 yards, but I would not take a chance on head shots beyond 8 yards with it. I wanted pinpoint accuracy in the event of a hostage being held close to a felon's head, and I did not trust the inverted Super-Vel bullet for that type of accuracy. So back to the drawing board I went. My wife saw so little of me when I was down in my basement shop experimenting that we almost got a divorce.

Finally, I decided to design my own bullet. Luckily, one of my shooting buddies was a top-notch machinist. I gave him my drawings and he made me a nose and base punch for my .38 Special swaging die. My design was a cup-point wadcutter with a shallow hollow base. I asked my buddy to make the nose of the cup point with the sharpest outer rim he could machine. I wanted this sharp outer rim because this was the configuration that penetrated best when striking a hard service at an oblique angle. The sharp edge on the cup-point nose would bite into the surface when it entered at an angle, whereas the tapered surface of a normal bullet would skid off.

I was greatly surprised by the accuracy test I conducted. I was able to hold 4-inch groups at 50 yards from a loose bench rest shot on the head of the B27 silhouette target. I was afraid if I dropped the weight down to 110 grains, the .38 bullet would not stabilize in a full wadcutter configuration. I was able to maintain bullet stability by designing a cup point in conjunction with a hollow base. This gave the light projectile increased bearing surface for stability.

I was also able to adjust the bullet weight up or down by adjusting the nose punch in or out. In the summer I used 100-grain bullet weights loaded to over 1,200 fps. During winter months, when heavier clothes were worn, I used 135-grain bullets traveling out at about 1,100 fps. I could have made them hotter, but I wanted lower recoil for faster follow-up shots.

I also produced this configuration for my stakeout partner, Bill Allard, who was an ace with his Colt .45 1911. We hand-fed the first .45 cup-point wadcutter, and we backed this up with a magazine of hollowpoint semiwadcutters. A week later, Bill saved my butt with that .45 ACP wadcutter with a one-shot stop.

I had confronted what was supposed to be two juveniles who had previously held up a certain hotel, always with their hands in their pockets. Bill and I had set up a plan with the desk clerk where he would use a code word when speaking to this juvenile team. When we heard the coded word, one of us would go out a side door and cut off their escape.

Sure enough, the clerk panicked and gave us the code word, only this time it was with a different armed team. As I slipped out the side door, what a surprise I received—both individuals were armed with autos! They both pivoted at my movement. The first gunman swung his weapon in my direction, but I dared not fire with a lobby guest directly in the line of fire. The gunmen then swung their weapons back and forth between me and the clerk. I yelled for them to drop their weapons. I knew the first character was doped up and wasn't going to let anyone get in the way of his next dose. As he swung his weapon back on me, I prayed that his shot would miss my unprotected neck and head.

My patented bullet compared to a Remington .45 ACP +P 185-grain hollowpoint. I designed the bullet so that it would only flatten out and not roll back into a mushroom ball like a hollowpoint. When a bullet mushrooms and forms a round ball, it only parts tissue, creating a small wound channel. Both bullets were shot into collagen tissue.

Side view of my bullet alongside the Remington .45 185-grain hollowpoint. Mine was a .45 ACP 178-grain full wadcutter slotted with a guide nose, allowing use in standard unaltered autos.

It seemed like an eternity before I saw the billowing dust and gun smoke pour out from behind the hotel desk and then heard the shot from Bill's .45. The first gunman reared up from a crouch, walked backward on his heels for about four steps, then fell backward. He was dead before he hit the hotel floor. The second gunman dropped his weapon and ran for the exit. Neither Bill nor I fired for fear of hitting pedestrians outside the hotel entrance.

At the postmortem examination, we saw that the .45 wadcutter had entered the gunman's sternum, clipped the pericardium sac, and come to rest along the left side of the spine. It had expanded to more than an inch in diameter. Had Bill used a standard .45 bullet, I probably would not be writing this book.

By now, I hope you have figured out the factors that I feel are needed to help increase a bullet's stopping power. Let's see if you agree with my findings. I will list them in order of importance:

1. Bullet construction and configuration
2. Bullet diameter
3. Velocity
4. Bullet weight

The last three factors are interchangable in terms of their order of importance, but they must rely on the bullet's construction and configuration. For example, with the proper construction and configuration, velocity could switch places with bullet diameter. For example, a 10mm wadcutter cup point of say 165 grains sent out at 1,300 fps will probably outperform a 185-grain .45 ACP wadcutter traveling at 1,100 fps. Of course given equal velocity, the larger bullet diameter would move up to second place again.

By now, have you detected a flaw in this chapter? Think about it. No, I am not advocating that we should only rely on revolvers. My sharp readers with good ballistic knowledge must be stating, "Is Cirillo nuts? Does he expect us to just hand-feed one cup-point wadcutter into our auto pistols?"

Yes, I agree that very few, if any, auto pistols can feed full

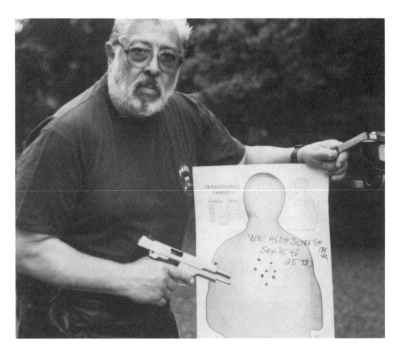

The results from shooting .45 ACP 185-grain Silvertips. Note the small puncture entries.

wadcutter bullets reliably. Think back, though. Do you remember I said I hid in my basement experimenting like a mad scientist? Well sure enough, I developed a means of reliably firing sharp, cup-point wadcutter bullets through semiauto pistols. Massad Ayoob first witnessed my demonstration in the late 1960s. I didn't pursue a full patent application then, as not too many agencies were using auto pistols. It is in the works now, though. Hopefully, the ammunition companies will pursue it if it proves to be cost-effective to produce. (The Pin Grabber people even worked with me and made some full-diameter Pin Grabbers for my concept in .45 ACP. Boy, did they work well. I wish I'd had them when I was in the stakeout squad. I would have named them Felon Grabbers. I hope to get them on the market someday. If I get enough of a response, I may just invest and produce them myself.)

Am I barking up the right tree? Is the cup-point wadcutter

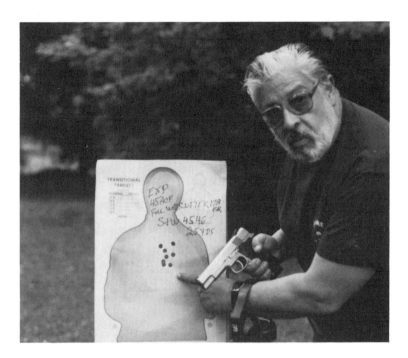

I shot my .45 ACPs out of an unaltered S&W Model 4546 double-action only. My patent allows full obtrusive wadcutters to flow through semiautos or full autos flawlessly. Comparing these entry holes to those made by the Silvertips in the previous photo provides graphic evidence of which round would be more effective.

with a sharp outer rim the way to go for a handgun bullet? At one time I thought the hollowpoint was the answer. I now know that the hollowpoint, if it does not plug up with clothing, may expand but only for a short duration; then it will fold back and become a large round-nose projectile. When this occurs the wound channel will be reduced, as any round projectile, no matter how large, only parts tissue instead of cutting and tearing as it traverses the target. Forensic technicians at the many postmortems I've attended have told me that they could not determine the caliber or the difference between a .32 or .45 bullet if round-nose bullets were used and passed through the victim because the round or tapered nose on the bullet parted rather than tore or destroyed tissue in its path.

In my estimation, putting a point or ogive on a bullet nose is analogous to dulling the edge of a saber. I know that traditionalists will say it is inefficient not to streamline a bullet, and this is true as far as long-range bullets such as rifle bullets are concerned. But with handguns used for self-defense, we are not much concerned with distances beyond 25 yards.

A second consideration is that very few, if any, defensive handguns can achieve the high velocities that contribute to rifle stopping power. Handgun bullets depend on mechanical rather than hydrostatic destruction. So velocity is a secondary factor in handgun stopping power; construction and configuration are the first.

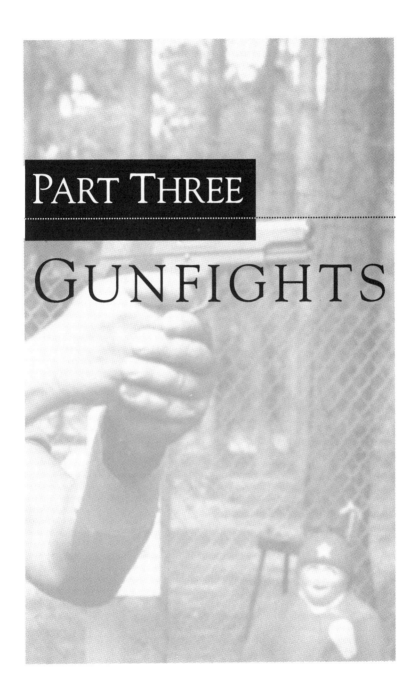

PART THREE

GUNFIGHTS

Chapter Five
SELECTION OF THE GUNFIGHTER

It must be one hell of a dilemma for police and the military to pick the right men for high-stress, high-incidence combat situations. As for the average civilian, I imagine many who legally have and carry handguns must also wonder what would happen to them if that moment of truth were to arrive.

How many of you have wondered if you could defend yourself successfully against an armed felon or felons? If this question has played on your mind, or if you are faced with selecting candidates for a specialized police or military unit, read on. You may find some hints in this chapter to answer your questions.

During the years I served in the NYCPD Stakeout Squad, I learned—the hard way—some streetwise lessons in the selection of a gunfighter. As a member of the unit, I spent about six years applying knowledge and theory of police firearms instruction in a practical manner. In this "school of hard knocks," one learned real fast both the shortcomings and feasibility of firearms teachings and techniques. I graduated from that school, walking away without a scratch from showdowns with 17 armed robbers.

I imagine that Mr. John Q. Citizen, while peacefully watching an exciting John Wayne western in the safety of his comfortable living room, is unaware that in this modern era of advanced technology, there is still a need for such heroes as pictured in those westerns—men who were then called "range detectives" or "town tamers" or whatever. These men had to be and were superb gunfighters.

I had the extreme good fortune to be present at the birth and development of a special unit in the NYCPD, a unit that, due to rare circumstances, evolved into one of the most expert groups of gunfighters ever assembled and trained in the history of the United States. One fact I am especially proud of is that I helped in the growth and refinement of this elite group.

At first I was reluctant when I was asked to join the Stakeout Squad, but my old competition shooting partner talked me into it. It all came about in the 1960s when there was a rash of robbery-murders of businessmen in New York City. Even after successfully completing the robberies and subduing the storekeepers, clerks, or owners of establishments, the callous gunmen would still murder their helpless victims. The business community was storming the doors of City Hall, calling for an end to the carnage.

Police Commissioner Howard Leary then ordered the formation of a stakeout unit. At the same time, because of a reduction in training due to budget cuts, expert firearms instructors from the police academy were being released back into patrol duties. I was one of those instructors. It was then suggested that the released firearms instructors sign up to form the stakeout unit. It was a logical choice, since the 70 men were superb marksmen with pistol and rifle, and many were top competitors in police and civilian pistol and rifle matches. In fact, two of them were national champions.

It was then that Lesson Number 1 was brought to light. Of the 70 men who were asked to join the stakeout unit, only nine agreed. I became number 10 only after my former teammate talked me into it. I was afraid of joining a unit I felt was destined to be exposed to a high degree of firefights. I knew I was a tough competitor when it came to shooting paper targets, but I wondered what would happen when my target could shoot back. It was probably the same question the other 60 considered when they turned down the invitation.

Lesson Number 1 taught us that just being a superb marksman does not necessarily make one a good gunfighter. Although we already knew that a good gunfighter must be an expert in the use of firearms, we now knew that a good gunfighter must also have some nerve.

Our police leadership went into shock when the 60 others turned them down. Their next move was to have the 10 bold ones (excuse me, I mean the nine bold ones; I was still holding my tail between my legs) act as both the nucleus of the stakeout unit as well as trainers for new candidates to be recruited into the unit. This is where I came into the picture. But first let's get back to how my partner conned me into joining.

When my partner saw my reluctance, he asked me, "How many times have you used your gun in your 15 years on the job?" I answered, "Just once." He then countered, "You probably won't use your gun for another 15 years. Come on, sign up. It will be nice and warm. They will feed you like a king. It will be a snap." So I signed . . . and in my first two hours, in the unit's second stakeout ever, I had to shoot three gunmen.

I never even got much of a chance to tell them to drop their weapons, as no sooner did I pop up to confront them when the groin piece of my bullet-resistant vest popped off and hit the floor with a resounding crash. All hell broke loose, and when the smoke cleared and the last piece of broken glass hit the floor, there was no one in sight.

I cursed myself, for just before the first shot broke I felt like I was coming apart. I thought I was turning into Jell-O and would pour right down the office steps into the store floor. I do not remember ever feeling fear quite so intense. But then, as I stood my ground and saw my sights, a very different kind of feeling came over me.

There now were two of me. One was full of doubt and

scared as hell. In fact, this part was questioning who was shooting the Model 10 S&W in my hand, for it saw the muzzle flash and felt the gun bucking. But the fear in me did not identify with the other part—the part of a man that is pure animal instinct, or perhaps more accurately, that portion of infallible subconscious mind that works faster and more accurately than a computer, that part of me which was saving my bacon.

At first I did not realize what I had accomplished. I thought I had missed. I was only partially relieved when I saw the first gunman lying down in the store vestibule mortally wounded. I hated the thought that the other two had escaped. In fact, they were on their way to a doctor's office to seek treatment for severe bullet wounds. They were arrested by responding police officers who had been summoned by the doctor's wife.

As it turned out, even though I was fear-stricken, I was able to hit all three gunmen in about three seconds. And that was with target areas of only 4 to 8 inches in width at a distance of from 60 to 75 feet. Never before or since have I been able to duplicate this feat.

This brought us to Lesson Number 2: a good gunfighter can perform under fear. In fact, he may even perform better with it.

Flushed with such quick success (in only 16 hours of stakeouts we nailed three gunmen), the department decided to use me as an example for the new volunteers. So we put our heads together, and with some knowledgeable supervisors also released from the firearms unit, we decided on a training and testing method to choose the other 30 members of the unit.

The NYC police administration then canvassed the entire department for volunteers to fill the 30 positions. This part scared me. I feared that some Walter Mitty types might worm their way into the unit, and one did, but he transferred soon after he soiled his underwear in a close call. I had worked with this type in the past, and it's bad enough when you have to worry about the gunmen, but to have to worry about the partner you're working with as well is just too much stress. Never pick a man who joins such a unit solely to prove his manhood. He's liable to blow away some imagined threat, if not you, in his haste to do so.

The selection committee did us a real favor—they let us

administer the crucible test to the candidates they felt had potential. We gave them various firearms tests, and we let the opposing candidates watch each other to put both peer pressure and the pressure of competition on them. This worked well, and it brought up Lesson Number 3: a good gunfighter has competitive spirit.

This spirit paid off for one of our selectees when he took on two robbers, both armed with sawed-off shotguns. He knew he had to hit the second gunman a crucial microsecond after hitting the first or we would be scraping him off the wall. Not only did he do this, but he told me that as he swung to the second shotgun-toting robber, he saw in his peripheral vision the first gunman still standing. He muttered a few curses at himself for missing the first gunman and prayed the man he had missed would miss him. He calculated, under all that pressure, that he had to continue to the second gunman, who was still surprised. He knew if he went back to the first man, the reaction time on the second man would be over and so would his life. As soon as he bowled over the second robber, he quickly went back and took a third shot at the first guy, who was now holding his shotgun in a port arms position. This time number one fell like a ton of bricks.

When the smoke cleared, Dave carefully walked over to ensure that both gunmen were in fact stopped, and, lo and behold, he could not believe his eyes. Right smack in the first gunman's chest were two perfect 12-gauge slug holes. He had not missed with the first shot.

I know you're shaking your head in disbelief. How can anyone take a 12-gauge slug and not fall? But as I mentioned earlier, I have personally seen men shot with 12-gauge slug, 00 buck, No. 4 buck magnum, 158-grain .38 Special round-nose, 158-grain .38 Special semiwadcutter, 200- and 230-grain .45 ACP hollowpoint, and 110-grain .30 carbine hollowpoint and still function. In my opinion, man is the toughest animal to stop. I had one gunman cock his revolver as I approached after a junior stakeout man had hit him with No. 4 buck magnum. The autopsy showed that his spine was severed, two pellets had pierced his heart, and five pellets had gone through his lungs. The only one-shot stops I ever saw were a 110-grain .38 Special Super Vel hollowpoint and a 12-gauge slug. Both were shots to the brain.

Empirically, we were learning what a gunfighter needed to survive: 1) extreme ability in accuracy, 2) plenty of nerve, and 3) competitive spirit, or the desire to win.

Some sad lessons were also learned. One factor that we were unable to test for at the time was Lesson Number 4: there are limits to each man's ability to take stress. We started getting men going sick with hypertension. Several had heart attacks, and one of my brother officers, whom I had trained and whose nerve and utmost accuracy I had lots of faith in, died in his sleep of heart failure at the age of 36.

It was only later that I learned that some of the men who had passed our test were suffering great stress. I had felt it during the first incident, but after my eighth armed confrontation I felt just a slight increase in heart rate, almost like hitting a home run when you know the game is tied and it's the last inning.

One of our best commanding officers noted some very important correlations that helped determine who would make a successful gunfighter. He wondered why some of the men were getting successful hits on stakeouts and why, even though some of the shoot-outs occurred under the most severe conditions (e.g., a crowded supermarket on Friday night), our men were able to hit several gunmen, while not one customer—not even a can of beans—got nicked.

The correlations unfolded like a map. They showed that the most successful gunfighters had some or most of the following qualities: they 1) were competitive shooters with a high degree of skill, 2) were successful hunters who got their quota every year, 3) loved firearms and collected them, 4) reloaded ammo, 5) loved outdoor sports, 6) were family men, 7) were outgoing and liked people, and 8) had great compassion for the underdog, including helpless victims of crime. When you think about these qualities, you can see why the men who had them were successful.

First, they were men who were top-notch competitive shooters, sure of their ability, who did not feel the apprehension that one with lesser proven ability would feel. That took a great amount of stress off of them.

The men who were hunters showed great patience because they could remain still for long periods of time without giving their presence away. They also had the nerve to wait out their game and not make their confrontation until they could ensure the safety of surrounding innocents.

Because these men had such confidence in their ability, they were not in the hypertense group. None of the men who were affected by tension had a hunting or competitive background. They had superb accuracy. They had nerve. But they still worried about their ability under pressure.

Those who collected firearms and reloaded had a good working knowledge of ballistics and firearms. This, coupled with our special training and their increased ability, gave them enough confidence to handle most gunfights.

The family man who had all of the above attributes was even more superior, for he took fewer chances. He wanted to go home. He wasn't about to let some beast of prey hurt him. He gave us safety and deliberation.

The outgoing, personable man with all of the above attributes who liked people and animals was topmost for safety. Many times, situations looked like armed robberies but turned out to be innocent. At such times, a man with no compassion might shoot when he shouldn't, or he might not consider bystanders during his moment of danger.

The two men in the Stakeout Squad who were the top guns and, as a result, were put into some of the toughest assignments, had most of the qualities mentioned above.

If you want to know if you fit the profile, or if you are a law enforcement official looking to select a special unit, here is a list of questions you can use:

1. Are you a competitive shooter?
2. Have you competed in major matches and placed and won awards?
3. Can you perform well under pressure or fear?
4. Are you a hunter? Have you shot big game?
5. Do you like outdoor physical sports?
6. Do you collect firearms? Do you reload ammo?
7. If you are over 28, are you married? Do you have children?
8. Do you like people? Do you attend civic affairs?

If you can answer "yes" to at least seven of these questions, you can make it. If you make all 12, you will likely walk away from almost any armed confrontation.

Remember one important fact: even if you fit the above profile in all aspects, you still must be able to train at least two hours per week, with someone else administering unknown judgment firearms courses under time limits and psychological pressure.

Chapter Six
SHOOTING FOR SCORE OR SURVIVAL?

To develop survival ability, many police officers enter pistol competition in order to enhance their shooting skills.

This is a step in a right direction, as the desire to win or at least shoot a respectable score places a degree of psychological pressure upon the shooter. This stress is somewhat similar to what one may feel in an actual shoot-out. Having been exposed to stress in both competitions and shoot-outs, I can speak with some authority on this comparison.

In order to achieve similar pressure and stress when I was training my NYCPD stakeout companions, I had them all watch each other's performance over a surprise course I had designed the night before. At his turn, each shooter attempted to better the score that had been fired previously. All the scores were then posted at the entrance to the stakeout headquarters. This placed a good degree of competitive pressure on my fellow officers. Nobody wished to be below the midway line on the large scoreboard visible to everyone.

This type of pressure training brought great results. In all of the gunfights that stakeout members engaged in, not one innocent person was ever hit by stray bullets. This included firefights in crowded supermarkets on Friday nights. Lt. Frank McGee, the commanding officer of the firearms unit, should be mentioned here, as he was good enough to allow us to conduct our own training. He knew full well that standard police firearms training would not fulfill the needs of a unit exposed to so many gunfights. Evidently our training tactics worked well. Not one stakeout member ever folded during any of the 252 armed encounters we faced.

We also encouraged stakeout unit members to participate in police combat matches. Our goal was to teach them that even though they felt stress in competition, they could still shoot accurately. We hoped this would maintain their confidence if and when they were involved in an actual gunfight.

If the competition allowed the shooter to do impractical maneuvers, however, I preferred that the stakeout member not participate. Let me give you some examples. In one match, the agency running the match provided the ammo. It also provided a brass bucket to eject the brass into in order to reclaim it for reloading. This was also done during the police department's qualification combat training. In the interest of saving time, this same department made each officer place and load 100 rounds of training ammo from the strong-side pants pocket.

Sure enough, one officer, when interviewed about a gunfight, stated that his revolver went dry during the firefight. He quickly reached into his pocket, came up with a dime, a quarter, and his car keys, and attempted to stuff them into his open revolver cylinder. He stated that he wondered what happened to his ammo. Who took his ammo? Why wasn't the ammo in his right pants pocket? He finally realized that his ammo was in the unfamiliar dump pouches on his gun belt. He fumbled for what felt like an eternity to snap open the pouch, and when it opened

When under Jeff Cooper's guidance, IPSC was geared toward improving techniques and equipment for survival. But like most sports based on war games, the desire for high scores has replaced the need for survival training, so practical weapons and techniques are no longer important. Although the weapon shown here built by Crawford Guns is a work of art, does it look practical for street work?

the rounds clumsily spilled to the ground. His opponent, who had already reloaded his weapon, witnessed the officer attempting his fiasco reload. Encouraged, he decided to rush in to get a better chance to shoot the officer. Either the officer was lucky, or there must be a patron saint who watches over police officers, because while he was in a kneeling position trying to recover his ammo, he was able to put just one round into the cylinder, close the weapon, and snap on two empty chambers before the live round fired. The gunman was only eight feet away and closing with his weapon pointed at the fumbling cop's head when the round tore into his chest and busted his spine. Felon 0; lucky cop 1.

Another officer from this same police department stated that he also went dry during a firefight. He opened his cylinder, poured the empty cases into his strong hand, and looked at his feet for the brass can before he realized there was none and that he had better dump the brass and reload quickly. Luckily by this time his opponent had taken off.

Now this is my point: under stress, you will do what you have been trained to do without even consciously thinking about it. Some call it an instinctive reaction, but I know it is a conditioned reflex that is ingrained into the subconscious through training. This conditioned reflex emerges when an individual is placed under great danger or stress.

An example of this is if an object were suddenly thrown at your face, you would automatically raise your hands to block it without any conscious thought to do so. This so-called reflex action was probably learned from infancy when something struck your face for the first time or when a sibling threw a toy or ball at you.

Again, my point is, if you attend pistol matches or firearms training that ingrain into your subconscious an improper tactic or maneuver, it may emerge under stress in an actual gunfight. Let me give you another example. In almost all International Practical Shooting Confederation (IPSC) pistol matches, a shooter will reload his pistol while on a run from one shooting barricade to another. Yes, it looks real macho and it helps the Comstock count score as it saves seconds, but is it sound tactics? In reality, I would load behind cover. If forced out into the open, I would want a fully stuffed weapon to have the option of returning fire in order to cover myself while on the run.

Another flagrant improper tactic: how many of you have witnessed some champion IPSC shooter stare at his weapon and holster while attempting a draw during a scenario? In real life I would be scanning the horizon to see if whatever is posing a threat has a backup ready to whack me out when my attention is drawn to the threat. In IPSC competition, they stare at the weapon in order to come up with a perfect grip during the draw since they know there will be no surprise threat.

As far as I am concerned, IPSC should be changed to ISC, as the word practical does not apply. I hope the IPSC reader does

In IPSC courses, the shooters load while running in order to increase their score by saving seconds. I teach students to load from cover so they would be able to shoot at their opponent if forced out into the open. It may take extra time in a sports match, but in reality it would save lives. To hell with the score!

A competitor shooting on the run.

not take me wrong. I agree it is a fine sport. I just feel that anyone who carries a firearm for protection should train and shoot in a truly practical manner. Of course, if you used a realistic approach during an IPSC match, you would lose a great deal in score.

In one IPSC match I participated in just before I dropped out of them, I ran up to a wall barricade. There were three targets: one 7 yards behind the wall, one 10 yards beyond and to the right of the wall, and one 20 yards beyond and to the right of the wall. I fired at the 10-yard target, then the 20-yard target, then reached around the wall and shot the 7-yard target. The range officer docked all my shots because I did not shoot the closest target. I argued that the 7-yard target had a brick wall between us, but the 10- and 20-yard targets could have taken me out as I reached around the barricade to shoot the 7-yard target. I suppose the shoe salesman and the plumber who designed the course only read the IPSC rule that the close target must be shot first rather than the most dangerous target. So much for proper tactics.

Some IPSC training courses actually teach students to look at the weapon before drawing it in order to facilitate a good grip. This can get you killed in the street.

At the same match, I ran up to another barricade and swiftly took out three targets. Again, I got tapped on the shoulder and the range officer advised me that all my shots were disallowed. I asked why. He replied that the right edge of my shoe had touched the foot fault line. My angry retort to the range officer was, "In all of my gunfights when I was a New York City police officer, I never had to look down on the ground for a foot fault line." I put my weapon in my holster, walked to my car, and never came back. When Jeff Cooper was the main honcho, there had to be a physical barrier to impose any foot or body position. Jeff made sure the word *practical* meant something.

Again, I beg the IPSC shooter to forgive me. I do not mean to criticize his discipline. I repeat—if you are shooting this for sport only and are not concerned about carrying a weapon for defense, continue to do so and enjoy an exciting game. I prefer to shoot the discipline the way Jeff intended—to prove which weapons, ammo, and tactics worked best.

At the Federal Law Enforcement Training Center, we went one step further. We allowed any caliber to participate, not just "minor" and "major" categories. This allowed from .380s to .44 Mags to compete. We also allowed any number of shots, as who can dictate to a shooter in a gunfight how many shots he should fire? Of course, we factored the time it took to fire those shots into the score, and we deducted points if you were exposed or loaded on the run. We also gave you a miss if you did not have at

This type of weapon is used in IPSC shooting matches. I wonder how anybody could conceal this gun for practical street use.

least a total of a 5-point hit on a target. The rationale was that your target was not incapacitated with fewer than 5 points. Our goal was to prove what caliber or weapon or style was best, which was Colonel Cooper's original goal.

We also said that any weapon could be used if it was truly concealable or was actually approved for duty use in duty equipment. I doubt very much if the present-day optical sights now used in IPSC would pass our concealability rule. I also have never seen or heard of a duty-weapon handgun in law enforcement with optical sights. I wonder about this. Is it because of fear that they may malfunction during a gun battle? If this happens during a match, you lose points. If it happens in a gunfight, you lose a lot more. With my eyes growing old, I know I could shoot much better with optical sights, but are they truly practical?

I wonder how many readers agree with me. Would you like to see a competition based on truly practical tactics as I discussed in this chapter? Would you like it open to any caliber?

This student successfully ran a fast-paced surprise assault course. The two outside targets pictured here were innocents who were shielding the felon (white target). A head shot was the only way to solve this rescue problem. During this course, no student knew what type of problem he would encounter until he turned a corner or passed into an open port. I design courses the same way that a gunfight can occur on the street—when you least expect it.

In my surprise course, the student is penalized if he does not use cover or if he gets tunnel vision and does not make acquisition on all targets, including innocents.

I was real proud of this disabled Vietnam vet who achieved a high score on a two-day course. Here he is going through a surprise house-clearing course. Note his good use of cover. The vet made it through without getting "shot" while rescuing family members and hostages. I like to work with handicapped people who have perserverance and work to overcome their disadvantage. Working as a safety officer on the left is the talented Marty Hayes of the Firearms Academy of Seattle.

This lady, fresh from spinal surgery, nailed every tight hostage-covered felon with centered head shots and made it through the surprise course with a high score using a H&K .45 ACP. I pity the mugger who thinks he's got an easy mark with this little lady.

Here is one idea I would like to see used. The host team would design a surprise match around a practical rationale. One of the visiting teams would also design a surprise match on an assigned basis. An equal number of targets would be used in both matches. Visitors would shoot the host's match, and the host would shoot the visitor's match. This way, the course would be a total surprise to each shooter. I prefer this, as in every gunfight I participated in, I had to play it by ear or sight. This system could provide three top winners: overall high score of both matches, overall winner of the visitor's match, and overall winner of the host's match.

If you agree with my concept, I would like to know. Write to me in care of the publisher. Perhaps we can correlate our ideas and form a truly practical shooting confederation. Until then, shoot realistically. You may not win a trophy or a medal, but you might just win a gunfight.

Chapter Seven: Firearm Training and the Gunfight

At this very moment in the United States, there are probably thousands of police officers on duty who hold their department's rating of expert in firearms. These same police officers are riding or foot patrolling their areas with total confidence that they will be able to handle any threat that comes their way. The expert medal they wear over their shield acts as a talisman to protect them. Civilians who have carry permits and attend approved handgun firearms courses may also feel that they can handle any armed threat that may arise. Their confidence comes from the instructor's certificate of qualification.

If the above training is all the police officer or the pistol licensee is relying on to protect him, then God forbid that he should ever get into a gunfight. If he does get in one and luckily survive, the difference between what he learned in formal firearms training and what he experienced during the real thing will be a revelation to him.

Even though I had supplemented my firearms training as a New York City police officer, it was a revelation to me. In the mid 1950s, the only firearm training for the New York City police department consisted of strong-hand dueling-stance single-action fire, bull's-eye slow fire, timed fire, and rapid fire. This definitely would have paid off if I had been slapped in the face with a glove and challenged to a formal duel, but even then I realized that this was not the way to go, so I supplemented my training with what I felt might be needed on the street. I purchased extra ammo ($1.50 a box at the time) and shot weak hand, strong hand, two hand, and double action. The range personnel looked at me with a cocked eyebrow as though thinking (probably rightfully so) that this kid was a gun nut.

In the next 10 years as a cop, I pulled my gun about a dozen times on duty but only had to shoot once. After much practice, I shot well enough to get into the police academy as a firearms instructor. At the same time, the NYCPD increased its training program with the new combat-style training inspired by the FBI PPC. I thought then that, compared to the old bull's-eye course, this style was the greatest thing since sliced bread.

In the late 1960s, when financial austerity hit New York City, the department stopped firearms training. The CO of the firearms unit dumped all the gun nuts out into the street and kept only those who had electrical or construction skills as firearms instructors. The first to go were two national police combat champions who had each won the national title two times in a row. I was out on the street right behind them.

During this period, as mentioned earlier, New York was suffering a rash of robbery and murders of businessmen and storekeepers, and the merchants were on the mayor's back to stop the slaughter. One of the assistant chief inspectors came up with the idea of starting a stakeout unit to combat the merchant robbery-murders. He stated, "What better way to staff it than to get 40 of the 70 firearms expert instructors out on the street to man it." They were shocked when only nine of the 70 were bold enough to volunteer. They did not realize that some instructors had wormed their way into the police academy because they disliked working the street. Volunteering for a unit with a guarantee of facing a high incidence of gunfights was the last thing they wanted to do.

Again, I must admit that I was not one of the nine initial volunteers. I knew I was a good shot, as I had won more than my share of pistol matches. I knew there was no silhouette target that could stand up to me. I annihilated those B27 and Colt silhouettes. I just wondered how I would react when the target was flesh and blood and shooting back!

Mike, my partner, who was one of the original nine volunteers, eventually talked me into joining. He told me that the chances of getting into a gun battle were extremely low. When he said, "Come on, Jim. They will wine you and dine you like a king," I succumbed and raised my hand and became the tenth volunteer.

Well, Murphy's Law caught me in my first stakeout. With just two hours on duty, I got into a gunfight with three armed robbers.

What a revelation. I was never so terrified in my whole life. They never told me in the academy that the targets were going to jump and move all over the place. There wasn't one 3' by 2' target to shoot at like on the police range. One gunman only gave me a 6-inch circle of his moving head to shoot at. The other two jumped behind the cashier and only exposed about 9 inches of their bodies on each side of her.

During those hectic microseconds when I popped up from concealment, my protective crotch piece fell off my bullet-resistant vest. I prayed that none of the gunmen would hit me in what I considered a most vital area.

When the metal nylon-covered crotch piece fell to the floor with a resounding clunk, all three turned toward the sound and pointed their handguns in my direction. The next thing I knew, I heard shots. I felt my Model 10 Smith & Wesson bucking in my hands, and I was asking myself mentally, "Who the hell is shooting my gun?"

When the smoke cleared, I did not see one gunman anywhere. I cursed myself for the fear that overcame me and was terribly embarrassed by what I thought was a total loss of control

I only have students shoot from the prone, kneeling, or seated position to take advantage of cover. Here I am pointing to bullet strike areas well in front of a target simulating a man in the prone position, producing ricochet hits on the target.

Compare my actual prone position to the simulated prone position of the target struck by the ricochet hits.

and accuracy. When the cashier told me that one robber was still there, I quickly drew my second revolver, but she stated, "Don't worry. He isn't going anywhere."

As I jumped down from the manager's booth where I was positioned, I was partially relieved that at least I had stopped one of the robbers. In fact, he was the one who had ducked and only offered a small portion of his head as a target. Boy was I glad I had supplemented my training by shooting for head shots and reduced targets. The department never made us do that in its training program.

When my watch commander showed up at the scene, I detected a tremor in his voice. He was a decent sort but was so nervous he could thread a sewing machine needle while it was running. At this time, a report came over the police radio that the other two gunmen were picked up at a doctor's office seeking attention for severe bullet wounds. This seemed to increase the tremor in the lieutenant's voice as he asked, "Jim, did you warn them? Did you tell them to drop their weapons and that they were under arrest?" I looked at him in amazement and disgust and replied, "Yeah, but I don't think they heard me because of all the shooting." As he walked away, I noticed a slight tremble in his walk as he tried to figure out my statement.

Now luckily my old partner Mike wasn't anywhere around. He was the one who said, "The chances of getting into a gunfight are extremely low." If Mike had walked in then, I would have punched him right in the mouth. I never felt so much fear in my life. I felt it was his fault that I was subjected to such danger because he talked me into joining the Stakeout Squad.

As I think about it now, I am very grateful to Mike. I received the Queen's County District Attorney's Award for Outstanding Heroism and later that year was chosen as one of the 10 most outstanding American handgunners. It was quite an honor standing up on the podium with such greats as Jeff Cooper and Elmer Keith, who won the first-place nomination that year.

Most important of all, however, I learned empirically how and what was needed to survive a gunfight.

No formal or informal firearms courses I ever attended came close to teaching me how to survive a real gunfight. In fact, some courses teach you to do things that may endanger you. Take the NRA Police Revolver Course, or what was once called the PPC. It still requires law enforcement officers to kneel in the open. To me, kneeling offers no advantage. It is unstable and a difficult position for mobility if the officer is charged. I only allow students to kneel to take advantage of available cover.

Prone is another dangerous position not only for its immobility, but even if an opponent misses the prone officer with a direct shot and shoots 5 feet in front of him, the ricochet will follow the ground and possibly strike the officer in the head. If he were standing, that same shot may only strike him in a leg or shin or pass between his feet. The seated position offers almost the same disadvantages.

The barricade position is another problem. In the Police Revolver Course, you must shoot from the weak side of a barricade with the weak hand. I teach my students to use the strong hand for both a right- and left-side barricade supported position. U.S. Customs adopted my style when I taught it as Chief Firearms Instructor in the New York region in 1976. It was later adopted by the U.S. Treasury.

Some firearms courses teach the seated position. This is what would happen if your opposition misses by shooting 5 feet in front of you. This was done on soft sand; on a hard surface, the ricochets would be more pronounced.

Note where I would have been hit by the ricocheted bullets had I been the seated target.

This is the way I teach students to use the strong hand on a weak-side barricade. I place the knuckles and fingers of the weak (support) hand on the flat back side of the wall. Then I cant the weapon so it will clear the wall, allowing the slide of an auto to function and the brass to eject without bouncing back into the action.

Even though I introduced the cant technique, the feds did not approve it. So this is the way they teach shooting from a left-side barricade with the right (strong) hand. I believe that you should never use the weak hand if nothing is wrong with the strong hand. Also, you expose too much of yourself using the shooting hand against the wall like this, and recoil against a rough wall can injure the shooting hand. I assume the feds only practiced this style against smooth range barricades rather than brick walls.

Note how much exposure the fed style of a strong hand on the weak side allows.

I developed what Massad Ayoob named the "Cirillo cant" back in 1976 when I was working with U.S. Customs. Canting like this allows better concealment, prevents the slide from dragging on the barricade, gives the brass clearance for ejection, and prevents the shooting hand from scraping against the wall during recoil.

Here is a strong-side barricade position with a .44 Magnum revolver. Again, the supporting hand will only rise off the barricade wall during recoil rather than scrape against it.

Another view of how little the shooter is exposed using my cant technique while shooting with his strong hand on a weak-side barricade.

Here the student is using the Cirillo "hammerhead shark" or what is also called the "slice of pie" method to peer around a wall. This technique allows a good view of what's behind the wall while limiting the shooter's exposure to a possible enemy.

I also convinced U.S. Customs and later U.S. Treasury to change from basic one-hand bull's-eye training to two-hand double action on a silhouette, with the bull's-eye scoring rings made hardly visible until the shooter was close up. This encouraged the student to aim center mass on a silhouette. Transforming the slow, timed, and rapid bull's-eye course into this style made transition into combat advanced style easy.

Various firearms courses that I've attended, even those run by internationally noted instructors, always emphasized to con-

One of my alternate sighting techniques is called the "geometric point." The weapon is held parallel to the ground and perpendicular to the shooter's body at the height at which he wishes the bullet to strike his opponent. This is used if the opponent is on the same parallel plane as the shooter. The shooter's main vision is on the opponent, and his peripheral vision is on the area where the weapon is pointing between his and the opponent's body.

If the searching officer/defender is surprised from the oblique, I teach the student to use the "nose point" by pivoting from the hips so that he points with his nose. By always keeping the weapon locked parallel to the ground and perpendicular to his nose, he can hit anything he looks at.

If there is distance, cover, or concealment between a shooter and an attacking opponent, the defender should by all means take advantage of using his sights if they are visible.

sciously seek out definite sight alignment. This is understandable to me because these instructors were never police officers. I assume they never drew their weapons at 4 A.M. or searched for an armed felon in a dark basement with only subdued light.

Also, would you dare raise your firearm to eye level if you turned a corner or entered a doorway and were surprised by an opponent only 3 or 4 feet away raising his weapon toward you? If you tried to seek definite sight alignment in this case, you could get the weapon snatched out of your hand or get shot using the precious microseconds to raise the pistol to eye level in order to see the sights. I encountered these conditions in several of my gunfights, but luckily I had trained myself to use alternative methods to aim a pistol accurately.

I do not want you to get the impression that you should never use the mechanical alignment of pistol sights. By all means, if the conditions are right, you would be foolish not to consciously seek out a sight alignment advantage. Sights should be used if you have cover, distance of 10 yards or more, and good lighting. Please

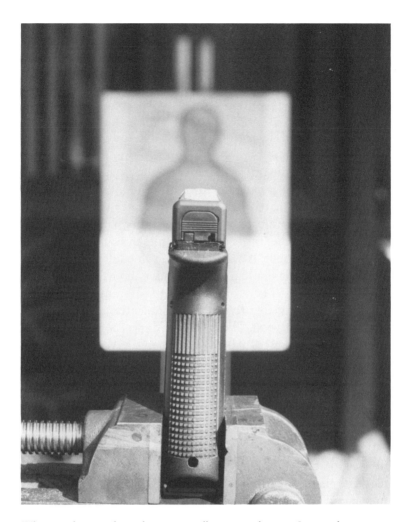

When teaching students the weapon silhouette technique, I cover the rear sight and have the student find what shape the weapon's rear silhouette looks like when the bore is perpendicular to the target. Shown here is a perfect silhouette indicated by the rectangular view of the slide without the sides or top of the slide showing. After the student ingrains this view into his brain through repetition and muscle memory, I remove the plug on the rear sight and have him rely on the weapon silhouette only, knowing he will now find the sights subliminally. This will be faster, and it will avoid snapping the trigger like many are tempted to do when they achieve a conscious view of a perfect sight picture.

note I use the word *consciously* for the above conditions. In my course, under certain conditions I teach my students not to consciously seek out the sights but to find them *subliminally*.

The subconscious has what many would claim are superhuman powers. Shooters who were able to use their sights subliminally shot 50 percent tighter groups with almost a 50 percent increase in speed. The reason for this is that the conscious mind is too distracted and harbors self-doubt. Consciously, you will take too much time trying to perfect sight alignment and may even snap the trigger when you think you have perfect alignment. Snapping the trigger will cause the shot to diverge, opening the group. The subconscious, on the other hand, only knows how to compress the trigger correctly while the sights are perfect. Since it has no doubt, it will not take up valuable time overcorrecting sight alignment like the conscious mind will.

I emphasize that subliminal sight alignment should be employed if the student is caught in close quarters within 10 yards and the lighting is good. The imminent danger zone is within 10 yards, and your chances of being hit increase as you decrease distance within that 10 yards. In close, the faster you can hit your opponent, the more you reduce that chance of being hit as you are forced closer into what I call the imminent death zone.

How I teach my student to achieve the subliminal sighting method is through one of my alternative aiming techniques. I call it the "weapon silhouette point." I teach the student to aim his weapon correctly; then I tell him to ascertain what the *rear silhouette outline* of his weapon is when it is aligned perfectly with the target. I then tell him to tilt his muzzle slightly up, down, left, and right so that he can see what his silhouette looks like when the weapon is aimed incorrectly. I then conceal his rear sight notch to prove to him how accurately he can deliver a shot using only a correct silhouette outline. When I taught this to one police department, I almost had to fight some of the students to make them remove the plug on the rear sight for the next exercise. They claimed they never shot as well as they did using the weapon silhouette method.

Can you figure out why some students shot tighter groups using only the silhouette point method? Think about it before

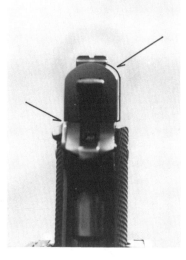

This silhouette indicates shooting to the left. Note the visible top left portion of the slide and the gap between the slide and frame..

This silhouette indicates shooting to the right. Note the visible top right portion of the slide and the gap between the slide and frame.

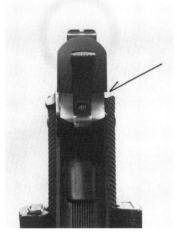

This silhouette indicates shooting up. The top of the frame is visible, and the gap between the slide and frame has disappeared.

This silhouette indicates shooting down. Again, the gap between the slide and frame is visible.

Here again is a perfect weapon silhouette with the rear sight taped. No portion of the slide is visible, nor is the gap between frame and slide.

When the tape is removed, you can see that the sights are also in perfect alignment.

you read further. If you can figure it out, you had proper basic firearms instruction.

Okay, let's see if you know your basics of marksmanship. The reason was that when using patridge sights, the sights appeared to wobble all over the target area. The shooter tried to pull the trigger only when he thought he had the sight alignment dead nuts to the target. He was trying to get only pinpoint accuracy, so he yanked the trigger when he thought he was on.

This caused two problems: anticipation of recoil, causing a downward pull on the weapon before the bullet emerged from the barrel, and a divergence of the barrel from the sudden forceful pull of the trigger. This combination of errors caused the bullet to hit wide of the target.

Now when the student could only see the outline of the weapon, he never was able to determine if he had pinpoint

This student shot these two-shot groups in a second and a half with his rear sight plugged up using the weapon silhouette technique. Some were shot one to the body, one to the head. He claimed he had never shot so well even with sights.

accuracy as he would with a sight picture using a patridge sight. As a result, he could not perceive any magic moment of accuracy, so there was no temptation to yank the trigger. Instead, he automatically squeezed it into a surprise break. This was sufficient to maintain a group of shots within 3 inches. Many knowledgeable firearms instructors will verify similar results with students who claim they shoot tighter groups in night fire courses than with full lighting when sights are visible. The indication here is that the student has had poor, or very little, basic marksmanship training.

I teach my students to use the weapons silhouette point under two conditions. Number one is when lighting is low and ambient and patridge pistol sights are not distinguished enough for sighting accurately. In poor lighting, the silhouette of the firearm is more readily visible compared to the minute patridge

FIREARM TRAINING AND THE GUNFIGHT

In my downed-officer defense course, students learn to shoot in any possible position they may find themselves in in the event they were hit first and downed. For example, they must shoot with their weak hand, strong hand, and two hands from the supine position, as shown here.

New York City police officers have been killed after being wounded and making no attempt to defend themselves once they were downed. Witnesses have stated that their assailants simply walked over to the fallen officers and continued shooting. In one case, the attacker, after his own gun went dry, actually removed the officer's revolver from him to finish him off. According to witnesses, the fallen officer had his hands upraised, begging the assailant not to shoot him.

sights. The second condition is when there's good lighting but there is imminent close-quarter danger within 10 to 5 yards. My reason for this is that I do not want my student to waste time seeking out his sights when the threat is so close. It takes precious seconds to consciously line up sights. Remember: the conscious mind harbors self-doubt, and it will use those seconds looking for pinpoint accuracy. The student then may jerk the trigger to try and snatch the magic moment, causing a diverged shot.

By using the weapon silhouette point consciously, I know that my student will subconsciously find the sights and react 50 percent faster and get off a shot with greater accuracy. He will not take up those precious microseconds to line up sights and be tempted to snap the trigger.

To accomplish the subliminal sight picture in training, the student is made to find the silhouette of his weapon that corresponds to an accurate point. I then neatly plug up his rear sight notch. After some dry fire drills, we go to live fire one or two shots at a signal. The student then does repetitive drills until it is ingrained in his brain to accomplish this subconsciously. When tight groups are achieved, we remove the plug on the rear sights and tell the student to work with weapon silhouette only and not seek out sight alignment. He is then tested under time limits.

In one class, my top shooter throughout the two-day course did not do as well as some of the mediocre or new shooters during the fast-paced subliminal-sight shooting test. I questioned him about it, and he admitted that he thought he would get 100 percent on the test if he sought out the sights for better accuracy. This actually defeated him because it cost him several misses. On the second half of the test, he did not consciously seek out the sights and his groups clustered tightly. He apologized for doubting me and noted that for being such a wiseass he was leaving with a score not as high as some of the novice shooters.

The message I wish to convey to you is that if you just want to shoot well or perform in competition only, the standard training courses, if well done, should suffice. If you are in a position where you might get into a gunfight, however, then you need training that addresses conditions that occur in gunfights. You must seek out firearms classes with instructors who have been there or who

I shot this head shot group from 50 yards with a double-action-only Model 4546 S&W to dispell the notion that double-action is not accurate in an auto. I prefer that officers use a double-action-only instead of a single-action or double/single-action auto. Only top notch shooters who practice frequently should use single-action autos. They are not for the average, poorly trained officer.

have been trained by instructors who have been there. Here are some of the firearms schools that offer such training:

>Massad Ayoob's Lethal Force Institute
>P.O. Box 122
>Concord, NH 03301

>Firearms Academy of Seattle
>P.O. Box 2814
>Kirkland, WA 98083

City Pistol Instruction
P.O. Box 110266
Campbell, CA 95011

Modern Warrior, Inc.
711 N. Wellwood Ave.
Lindenhurst, NY 11757

There may be other schools that address this type of training that I am not aware of. Wherever you go, ask about the instructor's background. Has he learned only through academia, or, as Col. Jeff Cooper puts it, "has he seen the elephant?"

Chapter Eight
STRESS OF THE GUNFIGHT

I am sure that any unseasoned law enforcement officer must wonder how he would react in a gunfight. When that moment of truth arrives, several reactions can be expected, but at that moment, one will learn of a particular miraculous reaction that can manifest itself when one is placed under great stress.

How many of you have heard stories of a woman of normal height and weight lifting an automobile off her child who has been run down or other amazing feats that under normal conditions would appear to be impossible? When we hear of such things, we tend to disbelieve them. I no longer totally disbelieve them. As a result of participating in several gunfights, I have vividly learned that people are capable of what may be considered superhuman feats when they are placed under extreme stress.

I mentioned above that several reactions may surface under the stress of a gunfight. These reactions depend on how the danger is presented. If you turn a corner and walk right into a gunfight, you will most surely react as you have been trained—and those are key words: *as you have been trained*. If your training was proper, you will dive for cover, as this is at the top of the survival tactics list. Drawing your weapon for defense should follow. If you react properly in this manner, you will probably survive this part of the gunfight.

Now a reaction called *fear* may appear. You may feel both physiological and psychological stress: the butterflies in the stomach, the wobble in the knees, a feeling of disbelief. This occurs as a delayed reaction to the gunfight that was thrust upon you instantly. This is normal due to the fact you were too busy protecting yourself and had many physical things to do. Your mind was required to think only of a defensive physical reaction. Once your mind is free from thinking of physical defense, it both releases all of the self-doubt you harbor and realizes how close to death you came. Then the fear sets in. I have spoken with many of my fellow officers who have also experienced this phenomenon.

If, prior to your first gunfight, you expect that gunplay is imminent, it can be a most horrifying experience. This happened to me in my first fight. It was evident by the actions of the four males who entered the establishment I was staking out that an armed robbery was about to take place. In these terrifying moments, I wondered, "Will I fail? Will I be killed?" Self-doubt played on my mind as terror and fear grabbed me. A feeling of great weakness came over me. I felt as though my limbs were coming apart and my bones were melting. I mentally cursed myself for feeling so much fear. When three of the robbers produced weapons and placed them to the heads of the cashier and manager, I knew that despite my great fear I had to challenge the gunmen before any harm came to the store employees.

As I popped up from concealment to make my challenge, I experienced a miraculous phenomenon. My pistol sights came into view as clearly and precisely and steadily as if I were at one of the many pistol matches I had attended. My mind had now committed the gunmen into blurs of color. Blue and Black melted into Gray as two of the gunmen jumped behind the cashier, who was wearing a gray shop coat. My pistol sights quickly shifted to gunman Green, as I dared not fire with the cashier acting as a shield for Blue and Black. Green had crouched down and was running toward Gray to use her as cover too. At this moment, a light or white object appeared in Green's raised arm. I asked myself, "Is he raising a white handkerchief in an act of surrender?" And at this very moment, I heard a shot and saw a blaze of fire emit from my pistol barrel. I felt the revolver bucking in my hand not once but several times, and I questioned myself as to who the heck was shooting my weapon. It felt like someone else was firing it. Green now disappeared. I shifted my attention to Blue and Black, both partially exposed on both sides of Gray. I then fired on both Blue and Black with intention. Blue and Black headed for the exit while Gray was frozen in her tracks, not ducking down as she was instructed to do previously. I fired again on Blue and Black, as they were both still armed and heading out the door. Blue and Black now were out of view, as was Green.

This whole action took only about three to four seconds, according to the manager. I could not believe this, as everything seemed to occur in slow motion. As the smoke cleared, I found Green dying near the cashier. I was partially relieved that I at least stopped one robber and was further relieved to find that what I thought was a white flag of surrender was actually a nickel-plated revolver with one expended shot that had buried itself in some cans of Planters Peanuts just in front of my position! Ten minutes later, information came over the police radio that two males dressed in black and blue clothing were apprehended in a doctor's office seeking medical attention for several bullet wounds.

I could not comprehend how I was able to take out three gunmen when I was so consumed with fear prior to the gunfight. I dared not speak of the strange phenomenon where I felt that someone else was shooting my revolver. Later, I understood that this miraculous reaction, which most probably saved my life, came from the subconscious. I remembered several times that I had felt a similar reaction in police pistol competitions. Once, as I walked off the firing line, everybody started to congratulate me. I wondered, "Why are they doing this?" I hadn't realized that I had shot an outstanding score or, for that matter, that others were shooting next to me. Again, it was the subconscious taking over due to the pressure induced by the desire to win, or not to lose, in competition. I now remembered that when I was under stress in competition, I almost always shot a very good or near record score even beyond my best practice scores.

It was now evident to me that the subconscious can take over during moments of great stress. When it does take over, it is infallible—it can only achieve perfection. The shots that I made in that first gunfight were so precise and so quick that I have never been able to duplicate the feat at a range on paper targets. (Jeff Cooper has incorporated a simulation of this gunfight into his training program and calls it the "Cirillo Drill." I believe Ray Chapman, another notable firearms instructor, is the only man who has been able to achieve this feat on paper targets successfully.)

I do not wish to convey to the reader that these reactions are unique to me or to rare individuals. I most assuredly know I am very normal. In fact, I consider myself, if not a coward, a man of normal fear and not really brave beyond the average person. All through my life, I've known many people who were much bolder and braver than myself, and I always admired their self-assurance.

By now you must be asking how I was able to perform such a feat if I claim to be so average. My only answer would be that from the first day one was given to me, I shot a weapon with great fear. I was actually scared of it at first, but I shot it in every conceivable position I could think of: one hand, two hands, weak hand. I knew that I had to learn to shoot this weapon well because my life or someone else's might depend on it.

Although I practiced diligently and frequently, at the time I was unaware of how my subconscious mind was committing all I was learning to memory like some supercomputer. As a result, during the gunfight, when my conscious mind went haywire with stress, the infallible subconscious came forth to save my skin.

The subconscious is there to protect us when it knows it must act faster than the conscious mind can react. All during our lives, we've been trained that objects flying in our direction can harm us. We probably were hurt by some early in life. It is now filed in our instant-reaction computer, the subconscious, to react in what we think is an automatic reflex action. But in reality, it is that miraculous reaction from our subconscious. If you had to rely on your conscious mind, a thought would have to register in the brain, then the brain would have to prod you to move your arms and hands to block the object. All this conscious thought takes time, which would not be fast enough to block it unless you were previously aware it was coming.

In all of my firearms courses, I strive to bring forth that subconscious reaction that I know students may need if they are confronted suddenly with the moment of truth. To the reader I say practice every chance you get, and gradually escalate the stress of the course until your confidence and ability grow. Get a buddy and design courses of fire that are unknown to each other. Push each other to react instantly and watch how, as the stress builds, the subconscious comes forth to help you achieve ability that would be difficult to acquire with the conscious mind alone.

If you are one of those blessed self-assured persons, your conscious mind will probably serve you as well as my subconscious did me in my first gunfight. Those people who are loaded with self-confidence will probably achieve perfection with almost everything they do—that is, if they were trained properly in the first place.

For the rest of us, once self-confidence is achieved by successful performance in succeeding gunfights, most of the stress factor will disappear. By the fourth or fifth gunfight, the most you may feel will be slight excitement—but that first one is the tough one! So train yourself well, and assure yourself with the knowledge that the fear and stress of the first gunfight can be overcome by your ability when it is enhanced by your subconscious.

Chapter Nine
THE BIZARRE NYCPD STAKEOUT SQUAD

It was the most controversial unit ever assembled by the New York City Police Department. Its members were the Green Berets and Navy SEALs of the NYCPD. Forty men were thrust into the most dangerous assignments devised for a police unit.

The Stakeout Squad was a unit within the NYC Emergency Squad. The Emergency Squad was a dangerous assignment in itself. When a precinct or a cop was in trouble, it was the Emergency Squad that was called for. They handled everything from airplane crashes to SWAT assignments. I was a member of the Emergency and Stakeout Squads, and it was the most exciting time in my life.

I loved working in both units and was proud to serve alongside such heroic police officers. I never considered myself exceptionally brave or courageous. In fact, I was somewhat ashamed of the feelings of fear that came over me in my first gunfight. Looking back at what I boldly did while in the stakeout unit, I questioned myself as to where the courage came from. Was it the courage of my comrades rubbing off on me, or was it the Greek Spartan blood of my grandparents flowing through my veins? My wife held a much lower opinion as to the reason for my heroic exploits. She told a concerned neighbor that I was such a coward that I would never even let the police department take my blood or stick a needle in me, much less let someone cut me or shoot my hide full of holes. I kind of prefer the other reasons for my acts of courage.

In many ways, being on the Stakeout Squad was a thankless job. It was started by a bold police commissioner, Howard Leary, but later came under an ultraliberal police administration. The liberal hierarchy condemned us as assassins, while the frontline police officers looked up to us as heroes.

It was the police bosses who had no knowledge of gunfighting who thrust us into danger. Had they listened to the expert gunfighters who made up the unit, we would not have had to resort to as many firefights as we did. But since we were only line officers, they let unknowledgable upper brass set up the stakeouts. They would put us in such close proximity to the robbers that we knew we would never recover in time if they decided to shoot first. We would not have the luxury of time to see if our armed robber would capitulate.

ONE INCH AWAY FROM DEATH

During training sessions, I instructed my fellow stakeout members to shoot if they did not see the robber throw down his weapon quickly when the officer made his confrontation and verbal warning. One of my men took offense to this instruction. He asked, "Are you telling me to murder these guys while I have a shotgun and a vest on?" I repeated, "If they don't drop their weapon the moment you yell at them to do so and they see your POLICE letters on your vest, I want you to blow them out of their socks." He shook his head in disagreement and did not speak to me for the rest of the training session.

Three days later this same officer challenged a robber in a liquor store on Second Avenue in Manhattan. He later told me, "Jim, you were right. I almost bought the farm." He said that at the moment he came out of hiding from the back of the liquor store and made his challenge, all he saw was a gun flash in the robber's hand as he quickly turned and faced the officer. One bullet struck the officer square in the vest over his chest. The instantaneous second shot passed just an inch past the officer's right ear and imbedded itself in the door frame behind him.

After he related the story, he shook my hand and apologized for doubting me. He then took a transfer form, filled it out, and left the Stakeout Squad. I forgot to mention that he quickly recovered after the second shot and started pumping the Ithaca Model 27 shotgun, blowing the gunman through the glass entrance door right out onto Second Avenue.

MARTY AND BENNY

I also had a comedy team in the Stakeout Unit, who I will call Benny and Marty. Ben resembled a muscular Lou Costello and Marty was the spitting image of Andrew Dice Clay and just as raw and funny. To this day I still wonder if they are related. During training sessions I tried to emphasize to them that at least one man had to be alert and on point at all times once they cross the threshold of a stakeout, but they never took me seriously.

The story that I am about to relate to you will seem unbelievable, but it is totally true. Marty and Ben were doing a 4 P.M. to 12 A.M. The stakeout was a drugstore in Brooklyn. Since it was near dinnertime they stopped to get a pizza. They walked into the drugstore with their takeout pizza, but instead of one man getting into the point position, Marty and Benny decided to sit at the back of the prescription counter and eat their hot pizza together, like the buddies they were. (The "point" was the term we used for the man on watch. In this case the point position was in the stockroom sitting on top of a phone booth. The phone booth was imbedded in the stockroom wall with its entrance flush to the store proper. It was a very good tactical setup. We always tried to get a high observation view.)

I can imagine the look on their faces, with a mouthful of pizza, when they spotted the upraised hands of the drugstore clerk heading their way. Right behind the clerk they saw the raised hands of the pharmacist moving toward them. They dove out of their chairs and scurried into the stockroom. As they waited, the robber herded the clerk and the pharmacist into the stockroom entrance. As soon as they were clear of the officers, Marty jumped out and pointed his Colt Detective Special into the middle of the gunman's face. He yelled, "Drop the gun!" The gunman responded with a shot fired right in the middle of Marty's gut.

Marty later told me that at that moment he thought to himself, "Cirillo's right. You will not feel the shot with adrenaline pumping into your system." Marty pumped six shots right into the gunman's face, and Benny joined with five shots from his Smith & Wesson five-shot Chief. Marty told me he saw the flash of the gunfire reflected in the gunman's eyes. He wondered, "When is this SOB going to fall?"

When Marty heard the dull clicks on his expended shells, he finally saw the gunman's eyes flicker and then shut as he crumpled to the floor. He yelled to Benny, "Benny I'm hit. Call an ambulance quick." Benny asked Marty, "Where are you hit?" Marty said, "In the gut. He could not have missed."

The pharmacist told me later that Benny helped Marty take off his shirt to look for the bullet wound. Marty had hair on his chest and belly as thick as an ape. He told me that when Benny was parting the hair, it looked like a chimp grooming another chimp. Benny now said to the ashen Marty, "I don't see any blood or a bullet hole." With a quivering voice, Marty said, "Geez, maybe it's in the belly button."

Benny asked the pharmacist for a swab. The pharmacist handed him a swab. Benny poked the swab into Marty's belly button. He took it out and saw there was no blood. Benny said, "Marty, there's no blood. Are you sure he hit you?" Benny then picked up and examined the gun that the robber shot Marty with. He laughed and blurted out, "Shit, it's a goddamned starter's pistol!"

Marty, still white with shock, sat down to recover. Benny got on the phone to report the shooting. He stood over the downed and evidently dead robber and called in his description. "I got a male black, 6'2" or 6'3", weight 270 or 300 pounds, age uh, uh, 32 years." With that the robber suddenly opened his eyes and said, "Shit man, I'm only 26. Hey officer, can I have a tissue? I got blood in my nose."

Benny's hair stood up on the back of his head, as he swore nobody could live with two revolver loads pumped into his head and face. Marty jumped out of the chair and felt his trigger finger twitching against an imaginary trigger. Then they both grabbed the gunman's hands and handcuffed him. He again asked for a tissue. Benny gave him a tissue. The robber blew his nose with a disgusting gurgling sound. As he blew his nose, a spent bullet fell out *plop!* to the floor.

The ambulance originally called for Marty now arrived. Benny was wondering, "How are we going to get this 300-pound gunman through the tight passage of the prescription counter?" He said, "Marty, we better call Emergency Service to get a body bag with handles to lift this guy." The gunman then sat up and told Benny, "Give me a lift, man. I'll get up." Benny and Marty pulled the felon to his feet. They supported him, fearing he might collapse. He pulled away from their grasp and started to walk to the ambulance waiting outside without the slightest wobble or any sign that he was injured.

Benny grabbed the gunman in the normal arrest mode and handcuffed him properly with his hands behind his back. Benny looked at Marty in amazement. They could not believe that this guy was so mobile with 11 shots in his head and neck.

At the hospital, Benny found out that not one bullet had penetrated the robber's skull. Each one had pierced the scalp, skidded around the skull and jaw bones, and exited. He later told me that he now knows I was right when I argued with the police hierarchy about how inadequate the 158-grain lead .38 Special load was.

THE TIMEX CAPER

My comedy team wasn't finished yet. These two characters still never took stakeouts seriously. No matter what instructions or advice I gave them in my training sessions, they still did things their way. They were so funny that I still, to this day, miss and love these two characters.

Marty and Benny were staked out in a chicken fry shop. Their scheduled assigned pickup was at 10 P.M., even though the shop stayed open till 11. At 9:55 they picked up their protective vests, broke down their 12-gauge Ithaca shotguns, and packed up their service guns and gear. They now were armed only with the same off-duty 2-inch Colt and Smith & Wesson handguns that they used in the drugstore shootout. As they were locking up the suitcase carrying their protective vests, they heard a voice coming from in front of the wall they were concealed behind state, "OK, motherfucker, I know dem cops is gone 15 minutes ago. Gimme all your cash or I'll blow your fucking brains out!"

Marty and Ben looked at each other in amazement. The thought running in their heads was, "This can't be real. It must be some stupid asshole making a joke." As Benny peeked around the wall, he could not believe his eyes. Here was a robber with a cocked .45 in his hand. He nodded to Marty, and they both popped out with their off-duty revolvers. The robber spotted them and ran for the door while raising the .45 in their direction, trying to cover his escape. Before he could drop the safety or fire a shot, Marty and Benny opened fire. Both aimed low on the gunman's butt to keep their shots heading downward. They were afraid of shots going parallel out into the dark street. The gunman toppled into a heap just before the store entrance. He lay there moaning and yelling, "Oh shit. You ain't supposed to be here. Oh shit. Goddamn." He was actually resentful that the cops were not playing by the rules and that it was unfair for them to be there. When Benny searched and handcuffed the gunman, he noticed that the Timex watch on the gunman's wrist was 15 minutes fast. Benny laughed, looked at Marty, and said, "Hey Marty, maybe we should call John Cameron Swazey and tell him Timex watches catch crooks!"

After this stakeout I always referred to my comedy team as the "Two Proctologists." (This stakeout also gave us new information. We found that whenever we shot gunmen in the pelvis or butt, they were knocked off their feet. They could still be dangerous, but at least their aim would be disturbed.)

THE BORN LOSER

This next occurrence I call the case of the Born Loser. It involved a sharp team that did as I asked. I will call them Kelly and Mac.

They had just arrived outside their assigned stakeout and were unloading their equipment from an unmarked car. Mac grabbed the case with their protective vests, listening device, and shotgun ammo. In his left hand he had a gym bag with his leather gear and service revolver. He started to walk to the assigned stakeout, an A&P supermarket, while Kelly was getting the shotguns and another equipment case out of the car trunk.

As Mac was walking toward the A&P, he heard a voice behind him that sounded as raspy as Louie Armstrong say, "Drop the bag, motherfucker, or I'll cut your ass." Mac turned around to see a large, muscular black man pointing an 11-inch knife at him. Mac jumped back as he swung the heavy suitcase toward the knife, attempting to knock it out of his hand. The case was too heavy to swing fast, and the felon was able to jump back before the suitcase struck him. Mac dropped his gear and quickly drew his Colt Detective Special. He yelled to his opponent to drop the knife. To his surprise, the robber yelled back, "Come and get it, motherfucker."

By now Kelly heard all the yelling and looked toward Mac and the big black man in a Mexican standoff. Kelly and the plainclothes highway cop who drove them there crept up behind the man, signaling Mac to be cool. They grabbed the robber by his pants cuffs and pulled him off his feet. Mac joined in, and the three of them did a sort of Irish jig on top of the felon until he dropped the knife.

Later that evening I called stakeout headquarters, and Kelly answered the phone. I asked, "Kelly, aren't you supposed to be on the A&P stakeout?" He then told me of Mac getting mugged as they were on their way into the store. Kelly then said, "Guess what, Jim? This is funny. This is the first day out of Sing Sing for this asshole. He just finished a 15-year term." I asked, "What did he get the 15 years for?" I heard Kelly chuckle over the phone. He then replied, "He tried to mug a cop!"

CIRILLO'S PUCKER FACTOR

I also had a close call in the very same drugstore that my comedy team was involved with, the one where Marty thought he got shot. I was seated on top of the telephone booth imbedded in the stockroom wall, the same watch point where my pizza eaters should have been when they were surprised by the upheld hands of the sales clerk and pharmacist. From my vantage point I could see who entered the store and approached the cash register. The sales counter was across the aisle, facing me.

A shady-looking individual who fit our hold-up man's profile entered the store. He went right to the pharmacist, who was behind the cash register. I could only see the back of this suspicious individual. He took something out of his pocket quickly. He had his back toward me, so I could not see what was in his hand, which was pointed toward the pharmacist. At this moment, the individual muttered some gruff, unintelligible words. The pharmacist quickly raised both hands over his head and said, "Don't get excited, don't get excited!" I aimed my revolver between the shoulder blades of the individual and took up 3 pounds of pressure on my trigger. I wanted to be sure there was a gun in his hand before I challenged him.

I was ready to take up the remaining 5 pounds of pressure on the trigger in the event he did not drop the weapon after my challenge. I whispered to my partner, "Bill, it looks like a hit." At that moment I saw the pharmacist bring down his hands, reach for what was in the individual's hand, and say, "I'll exchange it, don't get excited."

I felt my heart beating faster than usual and the adrenaline surge through my body. I don't know if it was caused by what seemed like a combat situation or by the thoughtless action of the pharmacist that placed a customer only 5 pounds of pressure away from death.

I was totally pissed off. I thought to myself, "I am going to teach this pharmacist a lesson." I told my partner to calm down, as I could see he was now experiencing an adrenaline rush. I explained to Bill what happened and told him to get the pharmacist and tell him I wanted to see him.

Sol, the pharmacist, came behind the stockroom and approached the phone booth I was sitting on top of. He looked up and said, "What's up, Jim?" I explained how close I had come to blowing away his customer. His mouth opened wide as he stated, "Oh my God." I then told him that if we had shot the innocent customer we would have covered it. He asked how. I told him, "We would have shot you and said he did it robbing you, and that would have covered us." Sol turned ashen white, walked back out to the counter, and for the next five days we were there he never raised his hands above his elbows. Bill and I laughed every time one of Sol's customers noted his restrictive movements and asked if he had bad arthritis in his shoulders.

BIG MOUTH

As members of the Emergency Squad stakeout unit, we were exposed to many bizarre occurrences. In order to offset the gory, catastrophic, and morbid scenes we witnessed, we learned to develop an abhorrent sense of humor to help shield our psyches. This was common among the members of the Emergency Squad, but it was not always appreciated by nonmembers.

One night on a graveyard shift I was working as an Emergency Squad officer between stakeouts. We got a call about a man under a train at a Brooklyn train station. When we arrived, the stationmaster directed me to the stopped train and showed me the headless corpse that had been dragged by the contact shoe and pushed between the train platform and the wheels of the train. I observed in the 3-inch space between the platform and the stopped train that the body was totally intact except for the head, which evidently was severed by the train wheels. The clothing on the body gave evidence that this poor soul was one of the homeless New York City derelicts attempting to cross the tracks to sneak into the transit system for a free ride.

By now a crowd containing civilians as well as local precinct cops and top brass had gathered. The stationmaster suggested that we bring the train into the train barn over the repair pits so that we could get under it and search the undercarriage for the severed head. I agreed. As the train rolled out of the station, passing over but no longer dragging the body, one of the local precinct officers shouted and pointed up the tracks about 100 yards to the severed head.

It was such an unusual sight. The head was resting upright, looking right at us, as though it had broken through the floorboards between the rails. Much to my and my partner's surprise, the precinct officer, in full dress uniform, jumped down from the platform and stated, "I'll get it." Without thinking, my big mouth came out with the humor normally reserved for and between Emergency Squad personnel. I looked to the crowd on the platform and said, "There's a young rookie cop who's going to get ahead on the job."

My partner turned his face away from the crowd to hide and suppress his laughter. When I saw the look on the faces of the crowd and the top police brass, I knew that my comment had gone over like a fart in church.

SO LONG NYCPD, HELLO FEDS

My best days on the NYCPD were when I was working with the Emergency Squad stakeout unit. The men I worked with were a different breed. Even though the job was sometimes dirty and almost always dangerous, we always had laughs and camaraderie.

When a Democratic liberal administration took over, the job changed. The men in the Stakeout Squad were accused of being trigger happy, and they pulled some of us out of productive stakeouts. One location was such a draw for holdup men we were popping out one or two a week. This bothered the liberal administration, because some of the holdup men were minorities. Soon after they pulled us out of that stakeout, a poor elderly salesclerk had her elbow blown off because she couldn't open up the safe fast enough. The stakeout unit members were furious.

When the liberal administration took over, my commanding officer was trying to get me promoted due to all the successful arrests and gunfights I had been involved in. At the inception of the Stakeout Squad, the police bosses promised the volunteers that after a successful shootout, the men who participated would be considered for a promotion to an assignment of their choice. My CO, however, had to apologize to me during a one-week period when my partner and I had to shoot four holdup men. He told me, "Jim, I don't know how I can ask you to keep on killing this way. I keep putting you in for promotion, but the brass never responds." Later I found out from buddies who worked with top brass that the liberal police commissioner had stated, "If we promote Cirillo, it would be telling all the young cops who come on the job that we promote cops who kill."

This same commissioner hardly ever did a tour on the street. He rode a desk as a clerical officer for all the years he was in the police department. The only promotion he gave me was to say, "Let's transfer him to a quiet precinct near his home. He has been much too endangered." In a way he did me a favor—he made it easy for me to leave the NYCPD and join the U.S. Customs as head of firearms training for Region II.

The feds treated me like I was the best thing that ever happened to them. After I took over and straightened out their firearms program, they gave me awards and promotions and pay increases. It was like a dream come true. What a difference from the NYCPD! In the police department it was microinches and microseconds—you were either a bum or a hero or dead.

With the feds I never left the firearms training range. Since I was a gun nut and in no danger of imminent death while pursuing my hobby, I had a ball. It was hard to believe that for all this I was given awards and praise.

I am sure the good Lord had something to do with it. I was compensated for a dirty, dangerous job by a much higher command than the New York City Police Department.

CONCLUSION

By now, you should have a good idea of what my book is about.

If you are in law enforcement or are a businessman who has a firearm for protection or a private citizen who can legally carry a concealed weapon or a housewife or single woman who keeps a firearm in the home, this book is geared for your survival!

The following are the most important points that I tried to get across throughout the book.

DO NOT RELY ON ONLY ONE SHOT TO INCAPACITATE AN ATTACKER

Too many people still feel that it only takes one shot to drop an opponent. Television and movies always leave the viewer with this impression. If you still harbor this belief, reread the story of Marty and Benny in Chapter 9. Eleven shots of .38 Special hardly caused any damage when shot into the felon's head and face from only inches away. Head shots are totally unpredictable.

THERE IS NO MAGIC BULLET

Yes, I had some instant stops on head shots in several of my gunfights. Some of these stops were due to my bullet design and choice of loading. I used sharp-nose wadcutters loaded to velocities to give me what I call bullet flight integrity. The problem is there are no commercial bullet producers that make such exotic ammo. These bullets were produced on Machinists & Corbin's custom dies made to my patented design. I then loaded them to velocities that gave the projectile enough flight integrity to maintain the bullet direction without veering off. In essence, I made my own custom bullets.

I tried for the best projectile configuration, construction, and bullet weight that allowed me to load to an adequate velocity. This gave me a combination of stopping power and muzzle control during repeated shots. I am hopeful that my patented design will become commercially available someday.

USE PROPER TACTICS

After reading "One Inch Away from Death" in Chapter 9, I hope I have made you aware of the importance of reaction time. In this case, even a trained police officer was under the false impression that he had the advantage wearing a bullet-resistant vest and carrying a cocked shotgun while covering a robber armed only with a handgun. Even though you think you have the superior weapon, you must employ proper tactics in order to protect yourself. Use cover, concealment, or distance. Cover should be able to stop the bullet. Concealment should make it harder for the opponent to get a shot at you. And if you cannot get cover or concealment, try distance. The greater the distance between you and an opponent, the less your chance is of getting hit. Try to stay beyond 12 yards. You are in danger within 6 yards.

One sharp Marion County, Indiana, Sheriff's Deputy and state-certified Survival Instructor, Keith Jones, came up with a concept he calls DCT, which stands for Distance, Cover, and Time. It's similar to my tactics concept except for Keith's introduction of time.

Time is another factor that should be employed to increase your chances of survival. If you're a cop, take your time getting into a gunfight, as time works in your favor, not your opponent's. In time, your backup will arrive. Citizens will call 911. Eventually, your opponent will want to get the hell out of there. So what if he gets away; at least you're going home safely. Your city fathers would rather you go toes up than have you shoot someone with relatives or the backing of a self-serving special interest group who will sue the city for political gain. So I repeat, use cover, distance, and concealment, and, as Keith Jones introduced, take your time. (Keith wrote a chapter on gunfight survival in Evan Marshall and Ed Sanow's book *Street Stoppers* on the latest handgun stopping power street results. This book, published by Paladin Press, provides very informative data on the ballistics of various commercial bullets. It's encouraging to know there are concerned researchers like Jones, Marshall, and Sanow. The efforts of these dedicated men should greatly increase the survivability of our law enforcement officers and lawfully armed citizens.)

TRAIN FOR PROPER BULLET PLACEMENT

I repeat: even though you may have selected the highest-rated bullet listed in *Street Stoppers* or some other source as the best stopper available, you still must be able to place the bullet where it counts.

There are two controlling factors that enable you to do so. One is the inherent accuracy of the bullet. The second is your marksmanship ability to take advantage of the bullet's accuracy. Once you have selected the bullet that gives you enough accuracy for your needs, it is up to you to train yourself to utilize the accuracy inherent in that bullet. I strongly recommend that you practice at regular intervals to achieve this.

If you cannot get to a pistol range, you can practice in your own home. I use a product called Beamhit America. It is one of the most effective training devices in my program. You place this laser unit in your weapon and shoot an accurate laser dot in place of a bullet. I actually taught my methods of alternative sighting and reduced-light firing in a hotel conference room using the Beamhit. The Model 110 system that I use costs about $500. You can easily spend much more on ammo and range fees and not get as much feedback as you can using Beamhit.

CHOOSE YOUR FIREARM CAREFULLY

You must choose a firearm in almost the same way you choose shoes for your feet or tires for your car—the firearm must fit your needs. If you're using an off-road vehicle, for example, you would put the appropriate heavy-duty tires on it. The same goes for choosing a firearm. If you're concerned with concealment, your firearm pick should be reduced in size and bulk but not in power. I would not use anything below a 9mm, and I would consider even a 9mm marginal and would try to use +P or better ammo in it. The Glock 27 in .40 S&W would be my choice.

In my own case, if I were still on the NYCPD Stakeout Squad, this mini Glock would be my second gun and the Glock 21 in .45 ACP would be my main weapon. My present favorite carry guns are a Smith & Wesson double-action-only .40 S&W and a Glock 23 in .40 S&W. I should say that these are my preferences; it does not mean that other weapons are not suitable for self-defense. My stakeout partner, Bill Allard, preferred his Colt 1911 National Match .45 ACP, and this was the weapon I wanted him to use. I knew he could make this gun talk. It spoke real loud when Bill saved my life with it.

It always galls me when I hear someone say, "Oh, that weapon is much too heavy to carry." To this I say, "When you get into a gunfight, you will wish you had the biggest, heaviest, largest bore handgun you could get your hands on."

HUNT WITH THE HANDGUN

Both my wife and I hunt big game with handguns. I use a

I've found that the mini Glocks shoot as well as their big brothers. I easily rolled nine shots out of this Model 27 .40 S&W.

Note the brass in the air and the absence of recoil as my wife, Mildred, fires this Glock Model 26. Glock did a superb job engineering these guns.

.44 Magnum Dan Wesson, and she uses a S&W Model 27 .357 Magnum with an 8 3/8-inch barrel. Mildred has taken seven whitetails with this handgun. We have scoped our handguns, and we use the Aim Tech mount system that allows full use of iron sights. We have found that it is much easier to use a handgun while up in a tree stand.

Bill Allard and I would go woodchuck or groundhog hunting with handguns during our stakeout days. We sharpened our skills on the varmints scurrying for their burrows. The dairy farmers loved us and claimed that we cleared their fields better than the varmint shooters with their scoped rifles. If you are in a unit such as SWAT or stakeout, handgun hunting is good training.

SUPPLEMENT YOUR FIREARMS TRAINING WITH MENTAL CONDITIONING

In the preface I stated that in the conclusion I would speak further of the most valuable piece of information for you to absorb from this book. It is the power of the subconscious mind!

It was my subconscious mind that came through for me when I was placed under great stress in a gunfight with three armed adversaries. My subconscious mind was firing my handgun within seconds with absolute accuracy while at the same time my conscious mind was wondering who the hell was shooting the gun in my hand!

I have experienced similar occurrences in stressful competition. The power of the subconscious mind is due to the fact that it only works in the positive. In other words, it will only perform what it has learned will work properly. That is why a falling human will place his hands in front of his face and head to protect his brain without conscious thought. What is called "instinctive" is in reality the subconscious working to protect us.

Under stressful conditions involving great danger, the conscious mind must overcome delayed reaction time and self-doubt. An example: if a heavy object is about to fall on someone, the time it takes the image to go from the eyes to the brain and from the brain to the legs to move is the reaction time. The self-doubt comes with such conscious thoughts as, "Am I moving in the right direction? Should I go right or left to escape the falling object?" This combination of self-doubt and delayed reaction time can cause enough hesitation to endanger the person under the falling object.

The subconscious will react in a fraction of the time that it takes the conscious mind to react. I became aware of this during those situations where my subconscious mind pulled me through. Afterward I realized that I should try to harness this ability to perform through the subconscious, so I started to employ different techniques in my training of students.

I used auto suggestion, speaking only in the positive. Instead of saying something like, "If you jerk the trigger you will miss the target," I would say, "As you focus on the sights while compressing the trigger smoothly, you will easily achieve a good shot." The results were outstanding. As a firearms instructor with the Department of the Treasury, I maintained a 93 to 94 percentile in my class averages, while the normal class average was about 87 to 88 percent. I was able to get high scores out of even the most apprehensive students.

When I retired from federal service, I was able to expand and experiment with subconscious training techniques, as I was no longer tied down with their lesson plans. I now gear almost all of my firearms training so that the student will react with an automatic reflex. I teach my students to find the pistol sights subliminally without being held back by self-doubting conscious thought. With conscious thought the student would take too much precious time trying to perfect the sight alignment. Also, when trying to perfect the sight alignment and sight picture, he may be tempted to yank the trigger, causing a missed shot.

You should try the weapon silhouette technique I described in Chapter 7 to work yourself into achieving subliminal sight alignment. Train yourself with repetition so that the subconscious absorbs the muscle memory into the brain computer for automatic reflex reactions. In the near future I will be making videotapes that will visually show you my training techniques.

Most important is to remember your tactics, distance, cover, concealment, and time. I would like to keep you alive, with the hope of meeting you in the future. God bless you.